KELLY COCHRAN. KILLER.

First edition. July 14, 2021.

Copyright © 2021 Stormy Barr.

ISBN: 979-8215328804

Written by Stormy Barr.

KELLY COCHRAN. KILLER.

Stormy Barr

Kelly Marie Cochran is undoubtedly a name that will be marked by history. On May 16, 2018, she was sentenced to 65 years in prison for the murder of her husband, Jason Thad Cochran, age 27, just one year after her life sentence for the murder of Christopher Karl Regan. Now the center of the Investigation Discovery documentary "Dead North," Kelly Cochran, age 34, has been accused of crimes beyond those sustaining her two sentences, including cannibalism and several other murders. According to Kelly's brother, Colton Gaboyan, Kelly might be responsible for the death of nine other victims across the states of Michigan, Indiana, Tennessee, and Minnesota. With the potential body count of eleven, Investigation Discovery has pointed out that Kelly may be "one of the most prolific female serial killers...of modern American crime." While Kelly is free to confess to these crimes without fear of incurring further charges, she has yet to respond to the accusations of cannibalism or to provide information on her other victims (though she has repeatedly claimed that there are indeed others). Now with the dismissal of primary investigator and Iron River Police Chief, Laura Frizzo, who had continued investigations into the possibility of Kelly's additional casualties, the case has run cold.

Kelly's infamous story begins in 2014, tucked away in the small town of Iron River, Michigan, with the murder of Chris Regan, age 51. Chris was a veteran of the Air Force and a father-of-two with an appreciation for the nature and climate of Iron River. Before his death, he was studying to get a business degree and had applied to a local mining equipment company. It was at that job that he first met Kelly Cochran, and the two began seeing each other. Though Kelly was married, this affair was seemingly just one among many. However, things changed when Chris' work was beginning to cause back and knee problems for him, and he applied to a desk job in North Carolina. Regan had just given his two-week notice at his job with Cochran when she invited him over to her home. This was unusual, seeing as the lovers usually met at Chris' apartment, but Chris agreed to go anyway, tempted by the promise of sex and lasagna.

A couple days later, Chris was reported missing. His abandoned car was found four miles east of Iron River, Michigan in a Park-and-Ride parking lot, according to reports at the *Rolling Stone*. Chris' on-and-off ex-girlfriend, Terri O'Donnell, explained that she knew something was amiss when he failed to respond to her messages regarding standing dinner plans. Regan and O'Donnell had been planning to celebrate his new job and explore the possibility of rekindling their previous relationship. After a few days, O'Donnell decided to go looking for Regan at the apartment he rented from her parents. She described the scene that awaited her to interviewers later.

"I open up the door, and the apartment was in shambles, it was a wreck, there was stuff scattered everywhere, there was dirty dishes all crusted in the kitchen sink," Terri said, "There was just red goo in the bottom of his wine glass. The windows were open, the apartment was cool, and his medication was all there. I mean he hadn't been there; he was gone. He vanished."

Terri proceeded to the Iron County police station to report Regan as a missing person; this is where Chief Laura Frizzo was first introduced to the case.

After speaking with O'Donnell and the human-resources director at Regan's workplace, Frizzo quickly deduced that much of Chris' time was spent with Kelly Cochran. Despite Frizzo's personal suspicions, the other detectives were initially hesitant to suspect foul play. Frizzo explained in an interview that the head detective believed "Chris Regan disappeared because he wanted to... he either killed himself or just disappeared." However, after discovering a slip of paper with directions to the Cochran home in Chris' car, uncertainty began to rise among the ranks of the police force.

Law enforcement soon visited the Cochran home, knowing she was one of the last people to have seen Regan. Once there, the behavior of both Jason and Kelly Cochran continued to incite skepticism regarding their involvement in the disappearance of Chris Regan. Initially, Jason tried to tell police that Kelly was not home. When she eventually came to the door, Kelly claimed that she had not seen Regan for a few days, even though no one had seen him in more than two weeks, and she even talked about him in the past tense. However, when their home was searched, the detectives found little to indicate the Cochrans were responsible for his disappearance. This distinct, conspicuous lack of physical evidence is often cited as an affirmation that Chris Regan was not Cochran's first victim, since most homicide perpetrators lack the presence of mind and foresight to successfully carry out that level of clean-up. Detective Ogden, who later interrogated Kelly, stated in an interview with *PEOPLE* magazine, "They were very thorough. Nobody's that good the first time around." After the search of their home in 2015, the couple moved to Hobart in Lake County, Indiana, leaving nearly all their belongings behind, including the food, furniture, and Jason's marijuana plants, according to Frizzo.

Despite the hasty departure of their prime suspects, detectives continued their search. After having minimal success at the abandoned Cochran home, they searched Chris' car once again. This time, a volunteer, retired Sergeant Michael Neiger, discovered some leaves stuck in the trunk of the car. This discovery was significant for two reasons: (1) the types of leaves could potentially indicate where the body was disposed of, and (2) Chris' apartment did not have any trees around it, but the Cochran home did. Furthermore, detectives discovered that the GPS device in Regan's phone placed him at the Cochran home on the same day he disappeared. Driven by their recent discoveries, investigators then analyzed Kelly's digital footprint and found images of Caspian Pit, an abandoned mining site full of dark, murky water.

The pit was searched, and divers were able to find and extract a burn barrel wrapped with a laundry cable fastened to a cement block. Investigators inferred that the barrel was the same one that was missing from the burn pit at the Cochran house; however, no concrete evidence substantiated the connection. With no more leads to follow, the case ran cold.

Meanwhile in Indiana, Kelly had begun a new affair with a woman, and the Cochrans had seemingly resumed their previous way of life. However, in February 2016, about 16 months following the disappearance of Christopher Regan, Jason Cochran was found dead. Initially, evidence seemed to indicate he had died from a heroin overdose. On the scene, according to Ogden and EMTs, Kelly's behavior was erratic and defensive; she was even described as "overacting." The FBI was also informed that the couple were suspects in another investigation, and an autopsy was ordered for Jason's body. The autopsy revealed asphyxiation as the cause of death, rather than the initially suspected heroin. Kelly fled to Kentucky, where she was later detained and charged on April 28, 2016 with the death of Christopher Regan.

Kelly's interrogation lasted for 70 hours and was conducted by law enforcement officers from both Michigan (for the Chris Regan Case) and Indiana (for Jason Cochran case). During the interrogation process, Detective Jeremy Ogden was able to extract a complete confession from Kelly. He staged a call where Kelly was led to believe Jason had left behind a letter to be sent to authorities containing information on their previous crimes; Kelly's confessions to the murder of both Chris and Jason soon followed. While incarcerated, Cochran temporarily cooperated with authorities and revealed the locations of the murder weapon, a long-barrel shotgun rifle with a .22 caliber bullet, and other tools used in Regan's murder, including a pair of forceps used in an attempt to extract the bullet from Chris' skull. She also led investigators to a site where officers were able to find Regan's skull and eyeglasses; however, parts of Regan's body are still missing. According to prosecutors, during this excursion, Cochran exhibited a distinct lack of distress and emotion, choosing to eat pizza and joke with officers.

During the interrogations, the events of 2014 began to reveal themselves. According to prosecutors, the Cochrans had created a "pact" during their honeymoon, which agreed that if either of them had an extramarital affair, they would kill the lover. While Kelly claimed that she had not taken the agreement seriously at the time, evidence indicates that she carried out the terms anyway. The night before inviting Chris to her home, Jason had confronted Kelly asking what she planned to do to "fix" their crumbling relationship. As a result, the two agreed to execute the pact and kill Regan. Court documents state that Kelly brought Regan to her home on October 14, 2014, where her husband emerged from the basement and shot the 53-year-old man under the pretense that he had "caught" the two lovers. Kelly provided the cord for the electric handsaw, which her husband then used to dismember Regan's body. During interrogations, Kelly referred to this process saying they had "downsized him" with a "big chisel." The couple then placed the pieces of Regan's body in trash bags and disposed of them in a wooded area in northern Michigan near Iron River. When they realized police suspected they were involved in Chris' disappearance, the couple fled.

When she was ultimately incarcerated, Kelly Cochran exhibited signs of violent and even psychopathic behavior. She used her glasses to create makeshift weapons and threatened to harm herself and others. Kelly also made several claims to indicate she may have other victims and opted to waive legal counsel. According to court documents, prosecutors began to doubt Kelly's "ability ...to appreciate the nature or quality or the wrongfulness of her actions or to conform her conduct to the requirements of the law." A preliminary investigation conducted by Melissa Powell, the Iron County prosecuting attorney, revealed that Kelly had previously been admitted voluntarily to a psychiatric hospital in Indiana from April 18-22,2016. Additionally, her findings confirmed Kelly's homicidal and suicidal ideations; the violent threats made during her initial incarceration stood as evidence. Thus, before prosecutors could bring Kelly to trial, her mental state had to be examined. Under the recommendation of a jury and Powell, Judge C. Joseph Schwedler ordered and expedited Cochran's forensic examination. After a brief waiting period, the results of the examination stated that Cochran was competent and thus fit to be tried for the murder of Christopher Regan.

Court documents state that Cochran was charged by the State of Michigan with "one count of Open Murder; One count of Home Invasion 2nd Degree; One count of Conspiracy to Commit Dead Bodies- Disinterment & Mutilation; One count of Concealing the Death of an Individual; One count of Lying to a Police Officer—Violent Crime investigation; and One count of Accessory after the fact to a felony." O'Connell revealed in a later interview with Fox News that when Kelly was finally brought to court "She just sat there and grinned," despite the extensive charges she faced. During the trial, Cochran pled not guilty to all charges, and instead attempted to place the blame on her husband for the crimes alleged against her. As a result of the trial, Kelly Cochran was sentenced to life in prison without parole by Iron County, Michigan in May 2017.

The interrogations following Kelly's arrest also revealed the circumstances surrounding Jason Cochran's death. The couple had gotten married in 2002 and made the infamous affair-pact while on their honeymoon. According to *Crime Watch Daily*, Colton Gaboyan, Kelly's younger brother, opposed the match and had expressed his opinion that "they just didn't fit." So perhaps unsurprisingly, while on trial in Michigan, Cochran claimed that her relationship with Jason had become progressively worse over the years. Contrary to accounts of family and neighbors, Kelly testified that Jason had become verbally abusive and had threatened physical violence. She even went as far as to call him a "monster" in her statement (a word she later used to describe herself as well). Supposedly as a result of their declining relationship, Kelly began having affairs with other women and men, one of whom was Christopher Regan.

Kelly indicated that her husband had pressured her into carrying out the "pact" and murdering Regan. However, during her statement in court, Kelly stated she "never stopped loving him" and recounted his marriage proposal according to the *Chicago Tribune*. The obituary published for Jason, reads:

Jason Thad Cochran, age 37 of Merrillville, passed away on February 20, 2016. He attended Merrillville High School and was currently a student at Purdue University Calumet studying Business Management. He was an avid fisherman and loved the outdoors. He is survived by his loving wife of 13 years, Kelly Marie Cochran...

It is unclear whether this image of the "loving wife" competing against an abusive husband is real or simply fabricated to garner sympathy.

After investigations began for the Regan case, the couple moved to Hobart, Indiana, and on February 26, 2016, Kelly placed a 911 call from their home on the 7100 block of Mississippi St. While on the call, she was recorded saying, "I don't know what's wrong. He's throwing up. He's sweating. I need an ambulance right away." When EMTs arrived on the scene, they were unable to revive Jason and initially assumed his death was caused by a heroin overdose. During this process, EMTs described Kelly's behavior as "disruptive," which, when coupled with her inconsistent statements regarding the events of that evening, led to rising suspicions of foul play. Those suspicions were later confirmed by the autopsy of Jason's body.

It was later revealed that Kelly herself gave her husband the fatal dose of heroin. She then cut off his air supply by putting pressure on his neck, nose, and mouth, causing him to suffocate. Detective Ogden described her confession saying, "she wasn't going to wait for him to die, it was taking too long... she wanted to show him that she had the power and she was in control." Kelly proceeded to have Jason's body cremated, against the wishes of her late husband and his family. After gathering evidence and getting her confession, the state of Indiana proceeded to charge Kelly with the death of Jason Cochran. The Chicago Tribute wrote that "His death was ruled a homicide by asphyxia by strangulation, complicated by heroin intoxication, according to attorneys." She claimed these actions were revenge for the death of Chris Regan and referred to the death of her husband as a way to "even the score." As a result of the ruling, Kelly was sentenced to 65 years in prison for the murder of Jason Cochran to be served consecutively with her previous life sentence for the murder of Christopher Regan. She took full responsibility for Jason's death, but Kelly has since appealed her first conviction.

Several people, including O'Donnell and Gaboyan, believe that Chris Regan and Jason Cochran are not the extent of Kelly Cochran's victims. However, as a part of her plea, Kelly cannot be charged by the State of Indiana for additional murders she may have committed. While she claims to have other victims, Kelley has thus far refused to give any identifying information or locations for them, leaving investigators uncertain of the validity of her claims. This distrust is exacerbated by Kelly's history and the rising suspicion that she may have psychopathic tendencies.

Kelly's personal background is rarely discussed due to the horrific allure of her crimes; however, some experts have pointed out that Kelly's past aligns with several known patterns of female psychopathy, which may explain some of her actions. During Kelly's trial, her mother, Melanie Gaboyan, described Cochran as having behavioral problems as an adolescent. Kelly began her drug usage in high school and repeatedly attempted to run away from home. After multiple therapists and placement in a girls' home, her parents reported that there was seemingly no behavioral change and eventually kicked her out of the house at age 18.

According to Psychology Today, it is typical for psychopathic tendencies to manifest during adolescence for women as they begin to manipulate their peers through flirtation, self-victimization, relationship aggression, and self-injurious behavior (for control rather than to relieve "intrapsychic pain"). However, Joni Johnston, a forensic psychologist and private investigator, explains that many teenagers exhibit similar behavior to Cochran and grow to be "conscientious, law-abiding adults," and even Cochran seemed to be on that path. Despite her continued drug use and repeated affairs, Kelly did successfully attain a college degree in psychology and earned the primary income for her household.

Underneath the exterior indicating positive growth, though, Cochran continued to exhibit a lack of empathy and a marked tendency towards deceit. During the murder investigations, Kelly made several unsubstantiated claims to have killed or injured numerous other individuals. Johnston used Kelly's false claim that "she had just killed a semi-truck driver in Illinois by stabbing him in the eyes" made shortly after he arrest in Kentucky and her "list of 21 alleged victims... [without] any identifying details" as evidence of her duplicity. This lack of honesty made for a difficult investigation process and continues to hinder efforts to understand and reveal the true extent of Kelly's crimes. Many of her testimonies were contradictory, which is what initially led to her becoming a real suspect in both Regan and Jason's murders. Even her mother questioned Cochran's ability to empathize, asking "Do you have a conscience, Kelly? Do you care about anyone? Because I don't think you do." Kelly herself is recorded as saying "You feel. And I can't."

Furthermore, Detective Jeremy Ogden, who was a part of the Jason Cochran investigation, described Kelly as being "manipulative, sadistic, calculative, and intelligent." These characteristics, paired with several testimonies from family members and detectives, have led to the general consensus that Kelly likely has other, undiscovered victims. Frizzo, the police chief who continued investigating Kelly's case after the convictions, has stated, "I'm so grateful that justice was served for Chris Regan, but I firmly believe that there are other victims out there." Since her second sentence, investigations have continued around Kelly Cochran. During the "Dead North" documentary interviews, one neighbor, David Saylor, revealed that Kelly had served burgers that had tasted unusual to a few of the neighbors, leading to the belief that Kelly Cochran may have served some of Regan's remains as a part of a neighborhood barbecue back in 2014. When he recounted the story, Saylor explained the meat did not taste like chicken or pork and even affirmed, "I believe we ate him." The documentary follows Frizzo and her continued attempts to investigate Cochran. It begins with the details surrounding the Regan case, which ultimately, according to Investigation discovery, led "down a rabbit hole that alludes to cannibalism, reveals human remains and uncovers a deadly love triangle." Continuing investigations were further complicated when, almost immediately after Cochran admitted to having other victims across the Midwest, Frizzo was fired by the Iron River City Manager, David Thayer. According to the Iron River Daily News, the Thayer regarded Frizzo's "management style and professional standards and practices as irreconcilable with his own." This decision was backed by the city council, which issued a statement saying, "under no circumstances would the council support reinstatement of Ms. Frizzo in her former position," according to Iron County's *The Daily News*. As a result of Frizzo's dismissal, investigations have gone cold, leaving the validity, locations, and identities of Cochran's other victims to remain shrouded in mystery.

Frizzo still works in Indiana, monitoring drug trafficking. She remains determined to have the Cochran case fully investigated and has expressed her desire to "follow through" on what she started. Frizzo has also expressed her concern that parts of Regan's body still have not been found, meaning there is no way to affirm if or how much he suffered before his death. This desire to continue investigations is shared by her partner, Detective Ogden, who told *PEOPLE* magazine, "At one time [Kelly] said that she had killed 21 people. On two occasions she told me that. I didn't believe it. I think that she was stretching things, she was just trying to play a game. She realizes that when she gives you 21 games, which she did, you're going to have to take time to look into them." Furthermore, he echoed the sentiment of many who have looked into the case saying, "I think there are others out there." Frizzo estimates that Cochran has "probably five" other victims, and Cochran's brother believes there may be as many as nine others.

Kelly's legacy continues to haunt the family and friends of her victims. Terri O'Donnell still mourns the loss of the opportunity to rekindle her relationship with Chris. She has been quoted saying, "We never had that opportunity to see if we could rebuild things or not. Kelly took that away." According to her statement recorded in the *Chicago Tribune*, "Right now, he should be in North Carolina with his son kayaking in the rivers and the mountains and hiking and biking and doing the things that he loved." Similarly, Jason's parents resent Kelly both for the murder of their son and her decision to cremate him. During her trial, the Powell read a letter from Jason's family to Kelly saying, "It was always about you" and "You are a very, very evil person." Despite Kelly's apology issued in her own statement, the Cochran family maintains that they will "never forgive" her, as said in their letter.

That accusation is seemingly corroborated by the *Post-Tribune*'s interpretation of a letter sent to them by Kelly Cochran herself shortly before she was found guilty for the murder of her husband. According to three different forensic psychologists, the letter demonstrates "self-pity narcissism." Handwritten by Cochran, the letter begins in a lighthearted, almost charming tone, asking editors to publish her story whilst condemning the reports from *Crime Watch* that portray her in a negative light. She signed the first page with the "i" in her middle name, Marie, dotted with a small heart. Katherine Ramsland, a forensic psychology professor at DeSales University in Pennsylvania, describes this peculiar opening saying, "She shows impatience and believes that her side of the story is not just important but is the only truth." Kelly even requests feedback, seeming to expect fans or followers who sympathize with her.

Kelly then begins her story in the second person, distancing herself from her own actions, and remains vague when referring to her crimes, omitting the names of her victims entirely. This section is brief and seemingly devoid of remorse. Portions are even pedantic, addressing the reader directly. For example, Cochran writes, "Don't run from something just to have to confront it years down the road when it's a big, mean, ugly monster." When she eventually switches to the first person, she only recounts her experience in jail. According to *Post-Tribune*, she gave "a timeline of her cases and how she's been kept in isolation." Her story contradicts accounts from law enforcement, and she describes her behavior in jail as "well-behaved and respectful." The letter ends with an attached drawing of two butterflies (likely mimicking her own tattoo) in front of barbed wire accompanied by the quote "The scariest prisons are the ones we create within ourselves." According to Ramsland, "The butterfly image suggests that she wants to present herself as fragile and helpless, caught up in brutal things that hurt her." These "brutal things" are likely, in Kelly's mind, her late husband that abused her, the drugs that altered her mind, and the judicial system that condemned her. Again, she signed the drawing with a heart above the "i" in Marie in the bottom right corner.

The experts working with the *Post-Tribune* believe that the letter was an attempt by Kelly to control the narrative surrounding her case. By portraying herself as a victim of circumstance and avoiding confrontation with her own crime, Kelly likely hoped to gain support from those following the case. However, despite this attempt to create a positive image, Kelly still refuses to reveal information about her other alleged victims or the whereabouts of rest of Chris Regan's remains. Thus, portions of the case remain buried in mystery, surrounded by competing narratives, sinister rumors, and the possibility of having American history marked by another serial killer.

TERMINATOR : THE TRUE STORY OF ANATOLY ONOPRIENKO

"I'm an angel who was attending a school of Satan. Some will call me schizophrenic or even Hitler or other terrible things. That's okay with me."
- Anatoly Onoprienko

CHAPTER ONE

Anatoly Onoprienko was born in the village of Lasky in Zhtomyr Oblast in the Ukraine on July 25th, 1959. His father, Yuri Onoprienko, was a World War II hero for the Soviet Union but according to Anatoly he was abusive and an alcoholic. He also had a younger brother who was thirteen years older than him.

His mother died when he was four years old and his father sent him to live with his grandparents and aunt. The grandparents subsequently sent him to an orphanage.

Onoprienko became bitter at his family and father for sending him to the orphanage. His older brother was allowed to stay in the family home while he was sent away.

"I remember my father and brother staring at me," Onoprienko said recalling his youth. "Staring at me saying, 'let's send him to an orphanage.' I don't blame them but I'm horrified by their memory. I remember their voices."

It is unknown why Anatoly was sent to the orphanage alone while his brother remained in the care of his father. His grandmother stayed with him for the first few days there, helping him to adjust. She would eventually leave but would visit often and bring care packages of food.

A shy and quiet young boy, he did manage to make friends inside the orphanage. He would play soccer and other sports. His grades began to decline, however, as he entered the college of forestry at age fourteen.

Teachers noted a shift in his personality and became concerned. He began drinking Vodka like his father and became involved in petty thefts.

Onoprienko left the college of forestry at the age of seventeen, still unsure of what to do with his life. He joined the army in 1976 and it is here where he mastered the use of firearms. Instead of becoming a good soldier, however, he became even more alienated.

"When I was twenty years old I called myself stupid because I couldn't understand people," Onoprienko recalled. "If they were smart then I must be stupid."

Onoprienko was discharged from the army then became a sailor. He gained employment on a cruise ship in Odessa and where he would often steal money from cabins. Despite his anti-social temperament, Onoprienko had a handful of girlfriends that he would try to impress with gifts purchased with money he had stolen.

One waitress on the cruise ship caught his eye and the two began dating. She would remain his girlfriend for three years and she would give birth to his first child. Onoprienko would take a stab at being a father for awhile but discovered that it wasn't for him.

Without a word, he left his girlfriend and his baby. Onoprienko would never see them again.

"I had a unique destiny," Onoprienko said. "I had to go out and find it. I felt restless at home. Stifled. Married life wasn't for me. I needed something more."

That "something more" would be crime and murder.

CHAPTER TWO

"Onoprienko's criminal activity would increase in 1989," Ruslan Moshkovsky (Onoprienko's attorney) said. "The USSR was collapsing and no one was responsible for anything."

Onoprienko's first murder would start with his landlady.

He broke into her apartment with the goal of stealing a few pieces of jewelry. The landlady, however, came home and demanded to know what he was doing in her house.

Onoprienko panicked and shot the woman dead.

He ran out of the apartment and continued on with his life as usual. Because the police resources were so stretched out, Onoprienko was never even questioned in the murder and the crime would remain unsolved.

Onoprienko would team up with a fellow petty thief, Sergei Rogozin, and the duo would break into various residences around Kiev.

Returning home from a night of thievery, the two spotted a car pulling a trailer late one night. Onoprienko sped in front of the vehicle, blocking its route then jumped out of his car with a sawed-off shotgun in hand.

A young couple was inside and Onoprienko fired upon them without warning.

"What are you doing?" Rogozin screamed.

"Shut up!"

"I thought we were just going to rob them."

Onoprienko sprang up in Rogozin's face, caressing his cheek with the barrel of his shotgun. "If you don't shut up...If you say anything, I will kill your entire family and make you watch. Do you understand?"

Rogozin could only nod his head in agreement.

Onoprienko then buried the bodies of the couple and set fire to their car.

A month later, the two thieves gunned down another couple using the same method. Onoprienko would speed in front of the car and stop. His victims caught unaware and defenseless, Onoprienko would spring out of his car and blast away.

Rogozin would say nothing and just take whatever valuables he could find off the victims.

Onoprienko would continue accumulating his victims in this manner. He would stop families on abandoned roads and kill everyone inside. Even children.

The home burglaries continued as well with Rogozin. Onoprienko killed a family of ten people when he and Rogozin were caught in the midst of robbing their house. Two adults and eight children were killed by the duo. Onoprienko then ceased all ties with Rogozin.

"He was a kind, intelligent man," Rogozin would say later of Onoprienko. "He wasn't greedy. He seemed good-natured. I cannot say anything bad about him."

CHAPTER THREE

Onoprienko kept a low profile for a few years, moving in with a distant cousin. There are six years in his life that are unaccounted for. Some say he spent some time in a mental institution while others insist that he may be responsible for more crimes in and around the former Soviet Union. He tried to get asylum in Western Europe but failed, returning to his native Ukraine.

"He worked in Germany and Austria," Dmitry Lipsky, the trial judge said. "During our interrogation we asked if he had killed anyone there. He denied it. He said he had only committed a robbery."

"At the very beginning, I had an option to commit suicide," Onoprienko said. "And to stop this mission to kill. But then with the passage of time there was an order from above that I cannot kill myself. I'm supposed to live and keep doing what I'm doing and finish this game."

Onoprienko would return to the Ukraine in 1985 and begin a killing rampage the likes of which his country had never seen. He had anticipated that his crimes on the highway would become the stuff of legend. Instead, they were forgotten in a bureaucratic quagmire.

Not only were his crimes unknown to the general public, no one was even investigating them.

The Soviet Union had collapsed and his native state, the Ukraine, was now an independent country.

"When he came back," Moshkovsky said. "And realized that everything had been forgotten and no one was looking for him, he embarked on his second killing spree."

Like a shark circling around a minnow of fish, Onoprienko moved from town to town surveying the lay of the land. He visited some relatives who were hunters and stole a shotgun from them.

Onoprienko would saw off the barrel of the gun in order to cause maximum damage. He wanted not only to kill again but to gain notoriety for the murders.

His new crime wave started with a seventy year old woman in Odessa. He broke into her home, shot her dead then set the home on fire.

"My main purpose wasn't to rob," Onoprienko said. "My purpose was cruel. I can't explain it. My purpose was to threaten people and threaten the police. And lead them in the wrong direction."

Days later, he would travel to a town called Malyn. He skulked around the town at night and come upon a young couple having sex in their car.

"I shot at them from the driver side," Onoprienko said. "I wounded the man then the woman jumped out of the car. I waited until she put her clothes on. Then she ran off. Probably to get some help."

The woman returned shortly thereafter to check on her lover. With Onoprienko hiding near the car, he stabbed her to death. He put the woman in the car, shot the man again then drove to a secluded area where he set the car on fire.

"I started realizing that there was a plan for me," Onoprienko said. "Something was giving me direction."

CHAPTER FOUR

Onoprienko began targeting families that lived in isolated areas around Kiev. He would follow the same modus operandi in each killing. He would create a distraction, usually throwing a brick through the front window to lure the adult male(s) out of the home. Then he would kill the man of the house before entering the home and killing the wife, saving the children for last. He would then set the house on fire in order to remove all evidence. There were instances wherein witnesses would cross his path and he would kill them as well.

Onoprienko was a nocturnal killer. During the day, he played the role of the down on his luck blue collar worker but at night he would seek out fame by being a serial killer.

He would move to a town called Yavoriv, moving in with a cousin named Pyotr and his wife Yelena. Ukrainian families were communal in nature and Pyotr saw it as his duty to take care of his struggling cousin.

Pyotr's wife Yelena, however, didn't like Onoprienko. She knew that there was something 'off' about the man and felt uneasy when she discovered the rifle under his bed.

Yelena pressured her husband into kicking Onoprienko out of the house. Pyotr could not throw his cousin out on the streets but he decided instead to play matchmaker. He knew a hair dresser that was recently divorced and looking for a decent man to be her meal ticket. Pyotor threw a family party, invite the woman over and she immediately hit it off with Onoprienko.

The woman was named Ana Kazak. She had two children of her own but her ex-husband was an alcoholic. She an attraction to the soft-spoken Onoprienko and the two began living together.

Onoprienko told his new live-in girlfriend that he was a "traveling businessman" and she never questioned his long absences from home.

Onoprienko would travel all the way to Malyn which was a town that was often hit by blackouts. He would be able to get in and out, do his killings under the cloak of night when no one had electricity nor did they have the capability to call for help. It was the perfect scenario for the serial killer.

CHAPTER FIVE

It was Christmas Eve when Onoprienko came upon the secluded home of the Zaichenko family which was located in the small village of Garmarnia. Inside, a forestry teacher lived along with his wife and two sons.

Onoprienko crept around the exterior of the home, found a ladder and propped it against the wall. He climbed up to the bedroom window and fired through the glass, killing the father and three year old son who was sleeping with him.

"I just shot them," Onoprienko said. "It's not that it gave me pleasure, but I felt this urge. From then on, it was almost like some game from outer space."

Onoprienko then jumped through the window and went from room to room.

"Don't kill us!" the wife pleaded as Onoprienko came through her door. He stabbed the woman and then strangled their three-month old baby.

"I didn't want to waste bullets on the weak," Onoprienko said.

He then ripped the wedding rings off the couple's hands as well as taking a small golden cross on a chain, earrings and clothes before torching the home.

Onoprienko would later say that he had "a vision from God" and was ordered to murder.

"When we arrived at the site, we were in shock," Leonid Martynenko, lead investigator of the Zaichenko murder said. "We discovered that the whole family had died violently. At the time, we didn't know the reason for the crime. We developed leads, examined a number of options. We considered burglary the main motive then. We thought it was homicide for purpose of robbery."

Onoprienko returned home and spent Christmas with Ana and her two sons. On New Year's Eve, however, the told her that he had to "go away on business."

Onoprienko would then travel to the town of Bratkovichi where he would indulge in his killing fantasies once again.

The streets of the town were deserted at night and Onoprienko was getting antsy. Then in the distance, he saw a man walking down the street.

"How you doing?" Onoprienko asked the man. "Was wondering if you could spare me a dollar or two so I can get something to eat?"

"Get the fuck away from me, you bum!" the man said. He was dressed in a forestry uniform and looked to be going home from work.

"Just a dollar."

"Fuck you!"

The man turned around and Onoprienko shot him in the back. The forester fell face first to the ground. Onoprienko quickly dragged the man to the side of the road. He rifled through his pockets, taking his money and keys. Then he stripped the man naked.

The night was just getting started for Onoprienko as he continued his rampage throughout the town. He noticed a man hanging curtains in his window and Onoprienko fired away, killing the man. Breaking into the home, he killed the man's wife and her twin sisters that were also living there. He then cut off the wife's finger and stole her wedding ring.

"It was like cutting through a tree branch," Onoprienko said. "It was very easy. Cutting through flesh was like cutting through butter."

He could not help but stop to admire his handiwork before he set the house ablaze.

"I was observing the victims," Onoprienko said. "Those who were already killed. How they were killed or were dying. Or how they were living the last minutes of their lives."

Onoprienko hopped on the train and returned home. When he got home, he took the wedding ring off the dead woman's finger and proposed to Ana.

"After the second murder we knew we had a maniac on our hands," Martynenko said. "We came to the location and viewed the scene. We saw the brutality of the crime and it had become absolutely clear to us that it was the same man that committed all the killings."

Gathering and sharing information still proved to be a problem in the Ukraine. Old Soviet style narratives were still being adhered to, like that of the government never admitting that serial killers existed in their country. It was part of the old Soviet style propaganda, wanting to prove to the world that killings didn't take place in their Communist territory. Even though the Ukraine was now free from such commandments, the leadership still adhered to keeping information away from the public and not admitting that they had a problem.

"It was striking how systematic the murders were," Romanyuk said. "There were group murders. Whole families were wiped out for no visible reason. That was really astounding."

Four days later after his marriage proposal, Onoprienko began gunning people down on the Berdyansk, Dnieprovskaya highway. He stopped cars, feigning as if he needed assistance then he would shoot the drivers. The victims were Kasai, a Navy ensign, a taxi driver named Savitsky, a kolkhoz cook named Kochergina and another unidentified victim.

"To me it was like hunting," Onoprienko said. "Hunting people down. I would be sitting, bored, with nothing to do. And then suddenly this idea would get into my head. I would do everything to get it out of my mind, but I couldn't. It was stronger than me. So I would get in the car or catch a train and go out to kill."

Onoprienko waited another eleven days, take a train to the village of Bratkovichi and invading the home of the Pilat family. He would shoot all five family members in the home and once again set fire to the place. He would be seen by two witnesses and he promptly killed them both.

"I look at it very simply," Onoprienko said. ""As an animal, I watched all this as an animal would stare at sheep."

The blood lust now running freely, Onoprienko could not refrain himself from killing.

On January 30th, 1996, Onoprienko killed a nurse named Marusina, her two sons and a family friend in Fastova, Kieskaya Oblast region of the Ukraine.

"I could not stop myself," he would say later to investigators. "I became obsessed with killing. To me killing people is like ripping up a duvet. Men, women, old people, children, they are all the same. I have never felt sorry for those I killed. No love, no hatred, just blind indifference. I don't see them as individuals, but just as masses."

Onoprienko would continue to take small items from the homes as souvenirs before going back home. He would bring his fiancee clothes, jewelry and a tape deck which he presented as gifts.

On February 19th , 1996, Onoprienko invaded the home of the Dubchak family. He shot and killed the father and son then bludgeoned the mother to death with a hammer. The family had a daughter, and he walked into her room to find her praying.

"Where do your parents keep the money!" he demanded.

The girl looked at her killer straight in the eye, defiant.

"Show me where the money is!"

"No, I won't," the girl said.

Onoprienko then killed the girl.

'That strength (the girl's) was incredible," Onoprieko said. "But I felt nothing."

Onoprienko then broke into the home of the Bodnarchuck family in Malina, Lvivskaya Oblast. He started with his usual tactic of throwing a rock at the door. The father, however, came out of the home with an ax. Onoprienko promptly shot the man and then the wife who came to the door to investigate the noise. Onoprienko then went inside and chopped up the daughters with the ax. A neighbor named Tsalk wandered onto the property and Onoprienko shot him to death before chopping up his body as well.

"Oh, you know, I killed them because I loved them so much," Onoprienko said. "Those children, those men and women, I had to kill them, the inner voice spoke inside my mind and heart and pushed me so hard!"

On March 22nd, 1996, Onoprienko shot and killed members of the Novosad family. He then set the house on fire to remove all traces of evidence.

"He would always set the places on fire," Romanyuk said. "People saw the fire and came to fight it. There was no evidence left only holes in the walls and cartridges."

Police would use forensic science to discover that the holes in the walls were left by a hunting weapon, specifically a gun that had the barrel sawed off.

"I'm not a maniac," Onoprienko said. "If I were, I would have thrown myself onto you and killed you right here. No, it's not that simple. I have been taken over by a higher force, something telepathic or cosmic, which drove me. I am like a rabbit in a laboratory. A part of an experiment to prove that man is capable of murdering and learning to live with his crimes. To show that I can cope, that I can stand anything, forget everything."

The Ukrainian government could no longer keep a lid on the killings. Rumors had spread of a man who was on a rampage throughout the entire country, murdering families at random.

The people of the region all lived in fear. Some families would stay together at night and press their furniture up against the door at night.

"People would come home from work early," said one Ukrainian resident. "People were scared to death. Students who were away at college quickly came home to be with their parents. I had one neighbor that put bars on their windows. Everyone was scared."

The press had given him the nickname of "The Terminator."

Onoprienko had achieved his goal. He had become the most feared man in his country.

CHAPTER SIX

The Ukrainian military patrolled certain villages to keep the people safe. Schools near the murders were shut down as a precaution. There was daily radio updates and a lot of the citizens likened the experience to being in a war.

"All the police departments were given specific instructions as to what to look for," Romanyuk said. "They knew how the killer behaved, that he acted at night. They investigated any sound. Even when a dog barked at night. The orders were strict."

The Ukraine launched a sweeping manhunt, determined to find the killer. They were convinced that this was the work of one man and dispensed their National Guard plus over 2,000 police investigators on the case.

"We had special teams of different officers working in different capacities," Bodgan Romanyuk, the chief of police said. "We had officers in the field, around-the-clock gathering information and working with operatives. Then there were others who in charge of strategy, who conducted the ground operations."

Later that month, the Security Service of Ukraine (SBU) and the Public Prosecutor's Office specialists arrested a 26-year old man named Yury Mozola, thinking he was responsible for the family murders. Over the course of three days, seven Ukrainian law enforcement officials tortured the young man, employing burning, electrocution and beatings.

Mozola, however, refused to confess and would later die during the torture.

The seven men were then prosecuted for the murder and sentenced to jail.

Days later after Mozola's death, Onoprienko was finally captured after a massive manhunt.

An anonymous caller gave police a tip on Onoprienko. He said that he witnessed him trying to conceal a shotgun as he left his apartment building.

Police then surrounded Onoprienko's building, staking out every possible exit until storming the apartment.

"It was quite risky," Romanyuk said. "Because on the one hand there was no evidence. But, on the other hand, what if it's him? What if it is this trained killer who shoots people dead on the spot and our officers are only human."

"We had learned that our suspect was anti-social. He wouldn't open the door to anyone. It was Easter and his fiance went to visit her mother, out of town. She would return in the evening and when we rang we'd hope that he'd think that it was her coming home."

The police came to the door and knocked.

Opening the door was a small man with red hair.

He opened the door calmly, expecting his girlfriend.

The police forced their way in and demanded his identification.

Onoprienko then reached for his gun but the police overpowered him, grabbing his wrists. Wresting the pistol away, they identified it as one that had been stolen from a crime scene.

Searching the man for his identification, they recognized him as Anatoly Onoprienko.

"In the apartment is everything," Romanyuk said. "All the evidence is there. Things from the crime scenes where he murdered people in different regions."

The police officers held up the numerous guns and knives to his face.

"It isn't mine!" the killer protested. "All that stuff doesn't belong to me."

His fiancee Ana, return home. She was shocked to see Onoprienko being arrested as she maintained that he had been the sweetest man she had ever met and had been nothing but nice to her and her two children.

The police, however, disputed her notions by showing her the weapons that he had stashed in her apartment.

"I started talking with his fiancee," Romanyuk recalled. "And I tried to find ways of connecting him with these murders. We were able to match dates. She would give us a date when he wasn't home for a day or two and that date would correspond with the murders."

The police searched through the apartment and found over one-hundred twenty-two items that were taken from the crime scenes. Guns and knives all matched what they were looking for in terms of murder weapons.

After the debacle with the previous suspect, the police authorities wanted proof beyond a shadow of a doubt.

"For me," Romanyuk said. "It was crucial that it we were sure that it was him. To make sure that he could be tied to these killings."

The police brought the killer into the station and interrogated him until six o'clock in the morning. Onoprienko denied all involvement until he finally cracked early in the morning.

"I was commanded by God to kill," Onoprienko told his interrogators. "I was chosen because I'm a superior specimen. I have the power of hypnosis and can call animals through telepathy. I can stop and start my heart with my mind."

He told of being diagnosed with schizophrenia and being admitted to a hospital in Kiev.

"He told us about all fifty-two murders he committed," Romanyuk said. "Not only the ones he performed in 1995 but also about the murders he committed in the past a long time ago."

Onoprienko expressed relief at being caught. He had grew tired of killing and being covered in blood all the time.

The police then turned Onoprienko over to the Ukrainian interior ministry.

Upon his transference to this higher authority, Onoprienko immediately began making demands.

"Give me a box of candy," Onoprienko said. "Sausages and some crackers. Otherwise I won't talk to you."

Onoprienko was then allowed to take advantage of a strange quirk in Ukrainian law. In the Ukraine, a trial cannot commence until the defendant has read all of the evidence against him.

At his leisure.

Onoprienko was obligated to read over volumes of police reports and crime scene photos. There were over fifty-two dead bodies, some dismembered and burned. Finally, he relented and after seven months he led the police to the areas where he had killed his victims. Onoprienko would detail each murder with an eery calmness, remarking at how easy it was for him to kill his victims.

There was another delay in that the Ukraine would have to transport, feed and house all of the witnesses who came from different parts of the country. Ultimately, there would be no witnesses testifying at his trial as some of the family members did not want to come forth.

A full three years after his apprehension, Onoprienko was finally brought to trial. Onoprienko was forced to sit in court in an iron cage. People spat upon him and threatened to tear him apart.

"I'm a person, a regular person," Onoprienko said. "Anybody can become a murderer. I was helped. It either it a God or the devil. Whatever he calls himself."

"He needs to be shot!" screamed a woman in the court room.

"He does not deserve to be shot!" screamed another. "He needs to die a slow and agonizing death."

The trial drew national publicity and the security around the courtroom was tight.

Judge Dmytro Lypsky asked Onoprienko if he had anything to say.

"No, nothing," the killer said shrugging his shoulders.

"You have been informed of our legal rights-"

"It's your law," he growled.

"State your nationality," the judge said.

"None."

"That's impossible."

"According to the police," Onoprienko said. "I'm Ukrainian."

"Do you have anything else to say in your defense?"

"I've been a robot for years," the killer said. "Driven by dark forces. I should not be put on trial until authorities can determine the force. You are not able to take me as I am. You do not see all the good I'm going to do! And you will never understand me. This is a great force that controls this hall as well. You will never understand this. Maybe only your grandchildren will understand.

Onoprienko was cooperative throughout the trial until the end. He requested that his state-appointed lawyer, Ruslan Mashkovsky, be replaced by someone who was "at least 50 years old, Jewish or half-Jewish, economically independent and has international experience."

The court refused his request. He was confined to a metal cage inside the courtroom as the rest of the proceedings took place.

"I started preparing for prison life a long time ago," Onoprienko recalled. "I fasted, did yoga, I am not afraid of death," Onoprienko said. "Death for me is nothing. Naturally, I would prefer the death penalty. I have absolutely no interest in relations with people. I have betrayed them. The first time I killed, I shot down a deer in the woods. I was in my early twenties and I recall feeling very upset when I saw it dead. I couldn't explain why I had done it and I felt sorry for it. I never had that feeling again."

The closing arguments began in April of 1999. Prosecutor Yury Ignatenko pressed for the death sentence while Moshkovsky would try to bring up Onoprienko's childhood to generate his sympathy.

"My defendant was deprived of motherly love since the age of four," Moshkovsky argued. "And the absence of care which is necessary for the formation of a real man. I appeal to the court to soften the punishment."

Moshkovsky himself, however, knew that Onoprienko was the epitome of evil, saying and doing things for dramatic effect.

"He was a cunning, shrewd and a great psychologist," Moshkovsky said later. "He was hard to catch because he acted alone and without accomplices. He was a butcher, killing defenseless and poor people. He specifically chose villages on the outskirts where there was no telephone, where even cars pass with difficulty. Even if someone heard a shot, there would be no one to call."

After only three hours of deliberation, the judge sentenced Onoprienko to death by shooting.

"I've robbed and killed," Onoprienko said in his final statement. "But I'm a robot, I don't feel anything. I've been close to death so many times that it's even interesting for me now to venture into the after world, to see what is there, after this death."

The Ukraine, however, had just joined the Council of Europe and had committed to abolishing capital punishment.

Onoprienko was then spared the death penalty even though he gave the President of the Ukraine a personalized letter that he would kill again.

"If I am ever let out, I will start killing again," Onoprienko wrote. "But this time it will be worse, ten times worse. The urge is there. Seize this chance because I am being groomed to serve Satan. After what I have learnt out there, I have no competitors in my field. And if I am not killed I will escape from this jail and the first thing I'll do is find Kuchma (the Ukrainian president) and hang him from a tree by his testicles."

The Terminator would die of heart failure in the prison of Zhytomyr on August 27th, 2013 at the age of 5

BRENDA SPENCER SCHOOL SHOOTER

JANET ERICKSON

In 1979, a five-feet-one-inch, eighty-pound sixteen-year-old girl would become the first school shooter in United States history. Brenda Spencer would open fire on Cleveland Elementary School, wounding nine children and killing two adults. Her assault would be the first of many school shootings across the nation, most notably Columbine and Sandy Hook.

The media and public began looking for answers as to why someone would commit such a horrid act. The response from Brenda was callous and flippant.

She hated Mondays.

But there had to be more to the story than that. Monsters are not born, they're made.

This is how the monster was created.

EARLY LIFE

Brenda Spencer was born to Wally and Dot Spencer in 1963. She was the youngest of three children, having a brother named Scott and a sister named Teresa. Despite being raised in a sunny San Diego locale, her family resembled something you would expect in a home of inbred hillbillies. Her saw-toothed father worshiped guns, allegedly committed incest and later married a minor.

Brenda's mother, however, would describe the home as a happy one before she initiated a divorce.

"He (Wally) was fooling around with other women," Dot Spencer said. "And he came home one night and asked me if he could leave for a year and if I'd let him come back. He'd already rented an apartment somewhere. I just laughed and a few days later I filed for divorce."

"That was just a rumor (his fooling around)," Wally said. "It was not true."

The divorce would hit Brenda hard. In her early childhood photos, she looked to be a happy child. Tiny but smiling in every picture like a normal kid. She enjoyed playing with her rabbit and spending time with her siblings.

"She (Brenda) was very active," Dot said. "She was always happy and a good child. Well-behaved. Never had any problems at school."

"After my parents got divorced it was like the latchkey kids," Brenda said. "It was like complete neglect."

Scott and Teresa opted to live with her father as in the 1970s era the court system allowed the children to have a say in picking the parent they wanted to live with.

Dot would lose custody of all the children, Brenda included.

"It (their custody battle) when the court system was swaying back and forth and he got the two older ones, they wanted to stay with him. And so they didn't want to split up the three so he naturally got Brenda."

"I went to court and I fought for custody," Wally said. "I loved my kids. I wanted to keep them, to raise them myself."

Dot alleged, however, that Wally wanted custody because he was too mean to pay child support.

The divorce would be the catalyst that would send Brenda's life into a tailspin. She became upset easily and felt invisible because her mother "was never around."

Brenda would claim that she would hardly ever see her mother and that when she did, her mother was indifferent to her presence.

"Sometimes I would stop by her house," Brenda said. "But she didn't seem to care to see us."

"That's not true," Dot said. "I'd see her once a week and then she'd come over and spend part of the weekend with me. I'd come home from work and she'd be sitting at the door waiting for me to come home. So we'd talk and what have you."

ABUSE...

Wally Spencer was a Navy veteran and a hunting enthusiast. He passed down his love for guns to Brenda, training her in marksmanship.

"She said she and her father had enough ammunition in the house for a small army," one classmate said. "Most of the boys and girls don't like her and won't go over to her house."

Wally worked as an audio-visual tech for San Diego State University. He had a steady job but for whatever reason, Wally elected to eke out a bleak existence. The furniture inside the home was sparse and allegedly they both shared the one sleeping mattress on the living room floor.

"I'd call him (Brenda's father) a loner," Dot said. "He didn't want to go to football games or baseball games. He'd just as soon stay home."

"The dad was a bitter man who hated the world," Brenda's attorney, Michael McGlinn said. "Her mother became a stone herself. You know, it was like, she never went out of her way to go over and see the kids, to have a relationship with Brenda so it was like a very cold, sterile environment in both places."

Brenda would later claim that she was both sexually and physically abused by her father which would be adamantly denied by Wally.

"I remember being hit in the face a lot," Brenda said. "Being hit in the ribs. Being yelled at, called names. I remember him coming home from work and being mad and smacking me in the head. And on different nights, he would just almost rape me. It was like that. Like he did. Like he would touch me inappropriately. I don't know how to say it."

Brenda would be asked as to why she never revealed this during his counseling sessions she would lie and say that she did, in fact, tell them about her incest but was ignored. During a later parole hearing, Brenda would claim to have been sodomized by her father.

"That never happened," Wally said. "I'll take a lie detector on that. That never happened."

During an interview with September Films, however, Wally came across as less convincing than his daughter when queried about the sexual abuse. He was asked if he ever molested his daughter and he raised his eyes in shock, looking like a bad actor.

"I don't have enough information to comment on the character of her father," District Attorney Richard Sachs said. "The only information I have is that she felt neglected by him and had accused him of sexual molest and forcing her to share a bedroom with him or bed with him. I don't know whether or not those allegations are founded or not. These are just things she (Brenda) has said."

"I had suspicions (of sexual molestations)," Dot said. "But she would never really tell me. The way she would be acting, very evasive if I asked her anything. It just wasn't her. I knew something was wrong."

HIGH SCHOOL...

Brenda began taking drugs in her high school years and became a truant. She turned to petty theft and shoplifting, staying home from school to watch any violent movie playing on television. She particularly enjoyed movies that featured cops being shot as she hated authority figures. Furthering her alienation, Brenda stated that she was "gay from birth."

Now a freckle-faced, red-haired girl who was impossibly thin, Brenda was noticeably different from the rest of her peers at Patrick Henry High School. She fell during a bike accident in her childhood and later tests would reveal that she had an injury to the front temporal lobe of her brain.

"This type of brain injury isn't uncommon among people who exhibit anti-social behavior," forensic psychologist Paula Orange said. "Brenda fell and hit her head. There are some instances where the injury is so severe that it changes a person's personality and outlook. Not making excuses for what she did but it could be part of the explanation of her personality changed to someone who craved violence."

She was described as "quiet" by most of her peers and some of her teachers thought her to be so introverted that they would inquire if she was awake.

But everyone thought she was harmless and no one thought she was capable of a mass shooting.

"She was never a violent person," Dot said. "I mean, (she) never beat up on the kids in the neighborhood or anything. Always very loving and caring and then all of a sudden she does something like this. It's hard to understand."

Despite her shy and reserved nature, Brenda did have some artistic ability. She was an avid photographer who had won a Human Society award for some of her shots.

Her passion wasn't shooting photos, however. It was shooting bullets.

"She wanted to blow a police officer's head off," said one classmate.

Brenda really wanted to kill a cop. She would have discussions with Brent, mapping out a plan where they would come up to a policeman sitting in a patrol car. Brenda would go to the passenger side window to distract him while her friend would shoot him from the driver side. She laughed as she talked about handcuffing him to the steering wheel then shooting him with his own gun. Another scenario would be for Brenda to lure him into a public restroom. She would throw eggs at his car and force him to follow her. Then once he set foot inside the bathroom she would kill him with an ax.

"She was always talking about guns," said another classmate. " Bragging about the guns her father had. She failed out of school last year (1978) and came back this year (1979. I didn't know her really well. I guess no one did."

Brenda would get expelled from high school due to her constant truancy. She was sent to a reform school who promptly informed her parents that Brenda was suicidal.

"Brenda was starting to have problems in school," Dot said. "They did send her to a special school. I had one interview with one of the people and they did say at that time that she was kind of suicidal."

Brenda's mother, however, never talked to Brenda about why she was suicidal.

"I figured her father would take care of her," Dot said. "You know, keep an eye on her."

Curiously, Wally would marry a seventeen-year-old cellmate of Brenda after she was jailed. Both parties refuse to reveal how the union came about.

"Sheila was her (Brenda's) cell mate in juvenile hall," Dot said. "She was released to go to a halfway house and she ran away from it. She went and got pregnant and they had to get married or go to jail."

The girl was younger than Brenda. People also marveled at how much she and Brenda looked alike.

"Her stepmother is younger than her," Dot said. "So they got married, had a daughter. Shortly after that Sheila left and left the daughter with Wally."

This revelation fueled the speculation that Wally may have been sexually abusing Brenda. When his daughter was incarcerated, he found a "replacement."

STARTING SMALL

The Spencers lived directly across from Cleveland Elementary School, less than one-hundred fifty feet away. Bored one weekend, Brenda would shoot up the windows at the school before breaking in and burglarizing one of the classrooms. She and a friend threw paint all over the classroom and overturned desks.

Brenda would be arrested and later released to her father's custody.

"She needs a lot of help," her probation officer said to the father. "I strongly urge you to admit her to a mental hospital. They'll take care of her, she's severely depressed."

"No," Wally said. "No hospitals."

Brenda would go on to have a "major fight" with her Dad. She absolutely refused to go to school because it was "boring."

Brenda's sister would later recall that she felt her father was too lenient with Brenda she would talk back to her dad. Brenda's sister did, however, say that her father made her "conform to the house rules." It became apparent, however, that when she challenged authority outside the home she would not get anything more than a slap on the wrist from her father.

BRING ON THE GUNS...

Brenda learned how to use a gun from her father and often bragged to other students on her prowess with weapons.

"She used to tell us how she went rabbit hunting in the mountains with a BB gun," said one friend.

"She'd shoot birds and cans," another classmate said "She had this long, straggly red hair. She was really scrawny, pretty crummy looking. She's a real little girl-real thin."

Deputy District Attorney Richard Sachs would later describe Brenda's appearance as "not like your typical sixteen-year-old. When you look into her eyes there is some type of emotional disturbance going on."

Brenda would become a truancy case, disdaining school and becoming a loner. She would skip school, take her BB gun to the local fields and shoot at small animals.

"She was different, that's for sure," a classmate said. "But she never really bothered anyone. You'd always see her walking around by herself at school."

With Brenda's anti-social behavior worsening, her father saw fit to give her a Ruger 10/22 semi-automatic .22 caliber rifle for Christmas in 1978. The rifle was equipped with a telescopic sight and 500 rounds of ammunition.

"He buys her a rifle with 500 rounds for Christmas," McGlinn said. "It's like 'Hello'!"

"I asked for a radio for Christmas," Brenda said. "And he bought me a gun."

"Why do you think he did that?" a reporter asked.

"I felt like he wanted me to kill myself."

Brenda immediately began practicing with the rifle. She placed all of her gun equipment in the garage, telling her friends that it would be her "fortress". She then dug a trench in the backyard and planned to use it as a "hideout tunnel".

"I'm going to do something to get on TV," Brenda told her friends as they saw the tunnel she dug in the backyard.

They were afraid to ask even though Brenda looked as if she wanted them to. She smirked at their fear and continued to dig the hole even deeper.

"I had failed in every other suicide attempt," Brenda later said. "I thought if I shot at the cops they would shoot me."

But her allegation of her father buying her a gun so that she cut kill herself is contradicted by her sister. According to Teresa, Brenda constantly badgered her father to buy her a rifle.

Strangely, her father would say later that Brenda never asked for a gun.

There was no record of any suicide attempts by Brenda yet she would talk about them in her letters after the shooting. She stated that the reason she could not kill herself was that she would "probably live, be a quadriplegic and be trapped even worse with Dad than I already was."

She wrote out a letter which explained why she did what she did.

"I want peace and see no other choice for myself."

Her father, however, found the letter and tore it to shreds.

DELUSIONS OF GRANDEUR...

Her best friend, Brent Fleming, recalled that day where Brenda had begun to dig the trench. He had accompanied her to shoot out the windows of the school and vandalizing it.

"Wait until Monday," Brenda told Brent. "Wait until you see what I'm going to do. It might even be big enough to make the news."

Brent recalled that Brenda's fantasies of being famous were not new.

"She stated on occasion that she would be famous," Fleming said.

The two hated all authority but with Brenda, it became the overriding theme of her life. Brent's mother recalled how they would sit around on the couch all day and complain about being hassled.

"They used to talk about what a rotten place the world was," Brent's mother said. "About how everybody hassles you. But nobody hassled them."

THE FATEFUL DAY

Brenda perched her rifle outside her bedroom window. She peered through the telescopic sights on her weapon and waited for the right moment.

Her heart began to race as the children stepped to the gates, arriving in groups of two or more. Brenda took a deep breath and squeezed the trigger.

Once she started, she couldn't stop.

January 29th, 1979 started as a normal day for Principal Burton Wragg. He stood in the front office, sipping from a cup of coffee while chatting with sixth-grade teacher Daryl Barnes.

The two then heard what they thought were a series of firecrackers going off outside.

Wragg went through the front door while Barnes went through the side.

Barnes turned the corner and found Wragg attending to a crying child on the ground. The principal then turned around and fall back into the bushes, blood on his chest.

Barnes grabbed as many children as he could, shoving them back into the front office.

"Call the police!" he screamed at the school secretary.

Running back outside, he rescued another child, hearing the shots ring out. He sprinted back to the office, looking back to see school custodian Mike Suchar coming to Wragg's aid with a blanket.

Suchar seemed unaware that there was sniper fire and was hit before Barnes could warn him.

"My God, I've been hit," Suchar said before falling to the ground.

A car full of children then drove up, equally unaware that a sniper was firing away.

"Get the car out of here!" Barnes screamed. "Get out!"

"It was a strange morning," Crystal Hardy, a surviving victim recalled. "It was just an eerie morning. There was frost on the grass. There was kind of a strange feeling."

"I remember walking to school by myself," Monique Selvig said. "I was about five feet from the sidewalk and then I heard firecrackers, the bullets that she was shooting go off. Then I turned around and faced directly across the street and got shot."

Her first shots wounded a couple of the children. Immediately taking action, the 53-year old Principal Wragg rushed over to protect the students, yelling at them to take cover inside.

"I looked out," Gaetana Payton, one of the schoolteachers said. "And the principal was flailing backward. And he had blood on his chest. And I thought 'Oh my gosh!'"

But another shot from Spencer hit Wragg and the Principal staggered to the ground. School custodian Michael Suchar rushed to the Principal's aid, trying desperately to drag him out of harm's way.

Brenda fired again, fatally wounding the heroic custodian.

The children scattered, screaming as Brenda fired away.

Robert Robb was one of the first police officers on the scene. He encountered a chaotic situation, children running and screaming. Two men on the ground bleeding.

Complete confusion and chaos.

"As we drew closer we could hear shooting," Robb said. "And as we arrived we could see a bunch of little school kids all huddled against the wall."

Robb exited his vehicle but was shot in the neck by Brenda.

"The bullet went in and it nicked my jugular vein," Robb said. "It bounced off my shoulder blade and lodged in my spine."

The spray of bullets would go on intermittently for the next fifteen minutes. Brenda would fire off a total of thirty rounds then barricaded herself inside her home. Police determined which house the gunfire was coming from and drove a garbage truck in front of Brenda's home to block her line of fire.

Authorities then began evacuating students out of the rear exit of the school. The children were then taken inside a school bus and driven to safety.

MEDIA COVERAGE AND CHAOS

A news reporter began calling homes in the immediate vicinity of the homes in the hope of contacting someone who could give him more detailed information.

He inadvertently dialed Brenda's number. The giggling sixteen-year-old admitted that she was the one responsible.

"I just started shooting," Brenda said. "That's it. I just did it for the fun of it."

"You may have killed three or four people," the reporter said.

"Is that all?" Brenda asked, her tone calm and matter-of-fact. "I have to go now. I shot a pig, I think and I want to shoot more.

Nine children would be wounded, one of whom was ten-year-old Crystal Hardy.

"I got shot and I was just waiting there," Crystal said. "Then I went to the nurse's office."

"The shot went through her wrist," Crystal's mother said. "Didn't hit the bone or anything. We're just praising the Lord."

"You're lucky," the reporter said.

"It was a very, very horrific event," Crystal said twenty-six years later. "My Mom just praised Jesus Christ because I was still alive. Certainly, it effected my life I mean it is something that traumatic would, of course, affect your life."

Nine-year-olds Monica Selvig and Christy Buell would be in critical condition. The bullet would exit through Monique's back, near her spine. Buell would be shot twice by Spencer, once in the stomach and her lower back.

Eight-year-old Mary Clark would be shot in the stomach as well, the bullet passing through.

"She (Mary) didn't tell anybody she was shot," a police officer said. "She just went back to her class. She was afraid to talk to anyone."

"I remember Crystal Hardy screaming," Selvig said. "Am I gonna die? Am I gonna die? Am I gonna die?"

THE STAND OFF

Police surrounded the Spencer home, shouting their demands through a bullhorn.

"I'll come out shooting," she said as police demanded that she surrender.

The SWAT (Special Weapons and Tactics) force arrived and staked out Brenda's home. They called her on the phone numerous times and she would simply hang up after a few tense words. Chester Thurston III, one of the primary police negotiators screamed through his bullhorn, ordering Brenda to surrender.

"I was irritating her like crazy," Thurston said. "I was squeaking the bullhorn. Basically raising all kinds of hell with her."

But Brenda knew what the protocol was for the SWAT teams. Her situation was playing out just like the ones she would watch on TV.

"She knew a lot about our operation from watching SWAT on TV," said SWAT member Mike Hendrikson. "She fantasized in the past about being a sniper."

The police would call back repeatedly and Brenda would alternate between being defiant and excited at the prospect that they would come and put her in handcuffs. Brenda wanted to get on television so her friends could see that she did "something big."

"Are there reporters outside?" Brenda asked.

"Brenda, you need to come out."

"Are there reporters outside?"

"Yes."

"And TV cameras?"

"Yes."

"Wow," she giggled.

The police realized that Brenda was home alone. They tried to appeal to her sense of family by asking about her parents.

"Do you have anything you want to say to your father?" the negotiator asked.

"Yeah," Brenda said. "Tell him to get screwed."

"How about your mother?"

"No. But I don't like her either."

After almost seven hours of back and forth, Brenda would get bored and surrender. Without warning, she stepped out of her home, placed her weapon down and gave herself up.

"I was a little pissed that the SWAT team didn't blow the whole house away," Robb said. "With her in it...I was shocked. To see this little girl, dressed up in what looked like army fatigues."

SWAT members would rush the home and find beer and whiskey bottles scattered on the floor. Brenda, however, did not appear to be intoxicated. She got into the police vehicle and was transported to the station, never saying one word until she addressed the media.

"I just started shooting," Brenda said. "That's it. I just did it for the fun of it. I just don't like Mondays. I did this because it's a way to cheer up the day. Nobody likes Mondays."

THE AFTERMATH...

Christy Buell would be hospitalized for a month after the shooting. She would then spend the next year and a half recovering physically. The mental aspect, however, would be a different story.

"There's no other way to say it," Buell said, her voice quivering with emotion. "I'll just never get over it."

Buell had lost her mother seven years earlier to leukemia and described her father's grief as "unimaginable." He had lost his wife and now faced the prospect of losing his daughter. Buell is also quick to remember the two men that were killed that day, Principal Burton Wragg and custodian Michael Suchar.

"The loss of two men that put their lives in danger to save children, that's the hardest part for me," Buell said. "The part no one will ever undo."

"I remember sitting watch TV that day," Principal Wragg's daughter Penny Buckley said. "And they are showing the same thing over and over again. Of course, it was everywhere, the news of my father (Principal Wragg) getting shot. And I remember sitting there, catching myself, anticipating Daddy getting home so I could tell him what happened."

Monica Selvig would get over physical aspect of the shooting but the mental trauma would always remain.

"She's evil looking," Selvig said years later after being shown a picture of Brenda. "I mean she's got these little glasses and those eyes. It is like something out of a horror flick. I mean I've never heard her talk but just she's eerie looking."

"I went to collect my Dad's things a couple days afterward," Buckley said. "And there was still blood on the sidewalk where he had died.

"It basically ended my career," Police Officer Robert Robb said. "It affected my ability to find a job. I mean I still dream about being a police officer and being out in the street. If I could I could go back to work tomorrow."

Brenda would be charged with two counts of murder and multiple counts of aggravated assault. Her trial had to be moved out of the San Diego area to Santa Ana in Orange County.

She did not find a sympathetic jury there, however. Brenda would be convicted on the murder charges and one count of assault.

Brenda would be sentenced to concurrent prison terms of twenty-five years to life (for murder) and forty-eight years (for assault with a deadly weapon).

Her "I don't like Mondays" comment would inspire a punk-rock song of the same name which was performed by the Bob Geldof and the Boomtown Rats. Geldof heard about what Brenda had done and then wrote the song in his hotel room.

"I tried to picture the girl," Geldof said. "I tried to visualize the scene: the police captains, the bullhorns, the playground, the parents. The girl must be some sort of automaton. And I wrote, 'The silicon chip inside her head gets switched to overload.' And, of course, why was she doing it? 'Tell me why?' May she's right. Maybe there is absolutely no reason. But it seems the California ethos didn't allow for reasons and logic for doing anything. They just did it."

The song would become an enormous hit in Europe but Colombia records became fearful of litigation from victims. They withdrew the song from radio airplay in the US after only a week.

"I don't like the Boomtown Rats," Brenda said when asked about the song. "But I like the song because it makes me feel famous."

PAROLE?

During parole board hearings, Brenda would later claim to be under the influence of both drugs and alcohol during the shootings. She recalled the SWAT members coming into her home, thinking that they were "commandos storming my house."

She would also claim that she had shot the people in self-defense in her deluded mind.

"I was watching TV and started drinking," Brenda said. "Whiskey and taking pills with it and I was smoking marijuana with PCP. And I started hallucinating. And when I look out I saw commando guys in combat gear coming up. Basically, I think I was trying to get myself killed."

This claim was repudiated by the arrest record as she tested negative for both alcohol and drugs.

San Diego Deputy District Attorney Richard Sachs said that Brenda is still psychotic and opposed her parole application.

"When her girlfriend was released from jail," Sachs said "She (Brenda) burned the words 'courage' and pride in her arm like a tattoo (she used a hot paper clip). She's still subject to depression."

According to Brenda, however, the self-inflicted tattoos do not read 'courage' and 'pride.'"

"It says unforgiven and alone," Brenda said, fighting back tears. "Unforgiven and alone."

Brenda as been open about her willingness to face the families of the people that she killed or wounded.

"They probably have questions," Brenda said. "It's not much, but it's the only thing I could do, answer some of their questions."

"I'm very sorry that I did it. I didn't have a right to do that to those people."

Brenda is now serving a 25-year-to-life sentence at the California Institute for Women in Frontera.

Her father remains her only visitor. He makes the five-hour round trip visit every Saturday from San Diego to Frontera.

"I don't feel responsible for what she did," Wally said. "But I still love her. She's my daughter and I still see her every Saturday if I can."

"I can't explain why she did it," Wally said. "I don't know."

Kathe Wragg, the widow of Burton Wragg, is a lot less lenient.

In her words, Brenda is "a pathetic, self-absorbed, bored, and uncaring thrill seeker" as her actions on January 29th, 1979 left innocent families devastated for decades after.

MISS RAMBO : THE TRUE STORY OF SPREE KILLER SYLVIA SEEGRIST

PAMELA SONG

She drank furniture polish.

She was obsessed with the military.

Then she shot up a shopping mall.

Sylvia Seegrist is unique among female serial killers in that she is the only one to shoot random strangers in a public place. While other killers of her gender seemed to have a certain motivation in mind, Seegrist was a paranoid schizophrenic that adopted more of a "masculine" attitude toward killing. She was a woman on a mission as she entered Springfield Mall in Pennsylvania and attempted to kill as many people as possible. The press would label her "Ms.Rambo" with her penchant for dressing in camouflage clothing.

EARLY LIFE

Seegrist was born in Pennsylvania on July 31,1960. She had a normal childhood and excelled in school by taken accelerated chemistry and math courses before her behavior became erratic in her sophomore year of high school.

Starting at the age of fifteen, Sylvia was hospitalized for various psychiatric ailments. Her mother would state that her mental decline began after Sylvia insisted that her grandfather had molested her. Rebellion set in and Sylvia had indulged in smoking marijuana as well as becoming the promiscuous girl around the neighborhood. She had to be removed from one class after causing a disturbance than she stabbed her high school guidance counselor. Placed in a mental hospital, she would attack one of the psychiatrists assigned to her.

Sylvia would grow to be a slight woman, with cropped black hair and a perpetual scowl on her face. At the age of twenty-one, Sylvia would be hospitalized in a mental institution for four months. When she emerged, her irrational anger and delusions were dialed up even higher. Her mother, Ruth, tried in vain to have her daughter permanently committed but the only way that could happen was if Sylvia engaged in a violent incident.

Sylvia would stay in her room and march in place as if she were a Marine private in basic training. Her mother would come in with her psych meds and Sylvia would often refuse to take them. She would salute her mother as if she were the drill sergeant and then slap the medications out of her hand. Her mother continued in vain to get Sylvia to take her meds but her daughter would too often refuse.

Then the erratic behavior would increase.

"Early sexual abuse can set off erratic behavior," forensic psychiatrist Paula Orange said. "But we only have Sylvia's word that she was molested by her grandfather. This could have been a delusion where Sylvia thought that something happened but in fact it really didn't. Schizophrenia happens in early adulthood so Sylvia was at the average age for which this illness takes place. She displayed all the signs with her disorganized speech, paranoia, and even her inflated self-worth as she would go into public places on go on rants about a coming nuclear war. A lay person would dismiss her as a crazy person but she was mentally ill. Her brain was not functioning and the girl could not do anything about it aside from taking her meds which she refused."

Exasperated with the state law requiring certain things take place before an intervention occurs, Ruth would argue to the mental institution that Sylvia had already committed violence and was a danger to herself and others. She recalled a time when Sylvia tried to choke her as they got into an argument outside the DMV. They would hospitalize Sylvia for three weeks after the attack but set her loose again.

"We were always fearful that maybe some tragedy would happen," Ruth Seegrist said. "She threatened it. 'I'll hurt somebody before I kill myself, I'll bring some people down with me.'"

"I felt homicidal off and on since 1980," Sylvia said. "I was angry at my parents for bringing me into the world."

Sylvia's mother, Ruth, was at a loss as to what to do with the now adult Sylvia. She could not live with her as that would put her own life in mortal danger. Her daughter needed supervision, however, because without it there was every possibility of Sylvia committing a violent act that would leave people dead.

"If the person is spiraling down into psychosis," Ruth Seegrist said. "Then he or she should be picked up by the police and taken to a hospital. There are other Sylvias. Walking time bombs, just as uncooperative and difficult as she was."

Diagnosed as a paranoid schizophrenic, Sylvia would bounce in and out of mental hospitals but never remain there like her mother wanted her to. Instead, she continued to be sent back into society. Dogged by paranoid delusions, she knew that her mother wanted her in a mental institution.

Sylvia wanted no part of that.

"She feared hat her medication was hurting her," reporter Reid Kanely said. "She feared that her family was out to get her and hurt her and sent her back to a hospital."

Sylvia would refuse to take her medication while in the mental hospital, spitting out the pills after the nurse would leave her room. Typical of a paranoid schizophrenic, Sylvia remained suspicious of any and all medication, especially when administered by a third party.

"She decided for whatever reason that the hospital was worse than prison," Kanely said. "And that in her twisted state of mind she would do something that would send her to prison instead of a mental hospital."

The voices in her head began telling her to do something. Something big.

Like shoot up a shopping mall.

"Having a child that is a paranoid schizophrenic is a horrible thing for a parent to go through obviously," Orange said. "The paranoid schizophrenic is the epitome of unpredictable. Furthermore, when Sylvia did wrong, her parents were blamed. And one can't imagine the heartache and hurt the grandfather must have felt when accused of molestation. These are delusions that schizophrenics go through. These delusions are rarely nice and without proper understanding can cause a lot of hurt. It can cause hurt even with understanding. It is a tragic disease."

A SCHIZOPHRENIC OBSESSION

Sylvia was an oddity in that she was obsessed with the military; guns, ammo, and killing. She tried her hand at joining the Army but was discharged because of her mental illness. The Army refused to comment further but clearly saw something wrong with the young Sylvia.

"Her obsession with the military is a bit odd at first glance," Orange said. "Because we associate military obsession as something that only men would be afflicted with. But with Sylvia the obsession with military power served as a coping mechanism. By her associating with the military she saw herself as a soldier in her own mind. No one would be killing her. She would be the one doing the killing, like a brave little soldier. The voices in her head told her that she was being attacked and her retaliation was justified. With this kind of obsession coupled with her paranoid delusions, Sylvia was destined to commit some an act of violence."

Her paranoia fueled this obsession. She pulled one of her neighbors aside one day and went on a bizarre rant.

"I had a dream," she said in wide-eyed wonder to the stranger. "Do you believe that dreams have meaning? I had a dream that I was a rubber ball. A rubber ball bouncing off the ceiling. What that means is that people push me around. Push me around because I'm different."

Sylvia was forced to live alone as she would do physical harm to anyone who was close to her. Away from any parental intervention, Sylvia spray-painted the walls of her home with sayings such as "kill 'em all" and "I hate you."

Around 1984, Sylvia visited a local McDonald's restaurant and began talking to herself. Staff became worried when she said that "someone should shoot up that mall" as she pointed her finger into a gun and went "rat-a-tat-tat."

"Sylvia may have been inspired by James Huberty who shot up a McDonald's near her hometown," Orange said. "She went into her own local McDonald's and said that she might do what Huberty did. This is what sometimes happens in the minds of serial killers and the deranged. When one person does a particular act, another person sees that as an affirmation for them to copycat the act. It started with Huberty shooting up a McDonald's which set off a mass of copycats similar to the school shooting epidemic in the 1990s and 2000s."

She then wandered around the Springfield mall on a regular basis, making bizarre comments and antagonizing shoppers.

"Your clothing is too bright," she said to one patron.

"Excuse me?"

"I said your clothes are too bright!" Sylvia screamed. "I hate bright colors!"

She would also go inside the stores and complain about the bright colors in and around the shopping center.

"It bothers me!" Sylvia would chastise whoever was listening. "Why doesn't it bother you?"

The bizarre behavior would scare numerous customers and clerks in the mall. Sylvia would be escorted out of the shopping center several times by security personnel and sometimes police. All the while, Sylvia would be simultaneously muttering gibberish and screaming obscenities.

"Get the fuck off me!" Sylvia would scream as the security personnel would strong-arm her out of the mall into a waiting ambulance. "I'll come back. I'll come back and shoot this place up. Just like Huberty. You saw what he did. He ain't nothing compared to me. Nothing!"

She would be sent to a local hospital for observation, sometimes being held for seventy-two hours after which she would be released on her own recognizance.

There would be no follow-up and Sylvia would return to the mall to repeat the cycle.

"The security personnel would see her as a nuisance," Orange said. "I don't think they saw her as a potential mass-murdering threat. Not that she would be perceived as harmless but she was just another schizophrenic who would pop up in the shopping center, create a scene, and then be ushered off the premises."

Her bizarre behavior would escalate over time. Sylvia would sometimes get up and rake leaves outside her apartment as early as four in the morning. She would march up and down the apartment building steps, high-stepping like a Marine soldier. Sylvia would go to the local health club and enter the steam bath while still dressed in her camouflage fatigues.

She would be a menace to any and all public places in the surrounding areas of Springfield, Pennsylvania. She entered one store in the mall and began drinking furniture polish. She would also frequent the public library, scaring more patrons.

"We're all gonna die," Sylvia said as she ranted and rambled down the hallway of the library. "The Russians. They're gonna nuke us all. And even if you survive there's gonna be radiation in the rain. It'll get into your brain. A big mushroom cloud over your house dripping poison on you. It's over. They say it won't happen but it will. Trust me."

In March of 1985, she would enter a K-mart dressed in military fatigues. She would insist on the purchase of a rifle but was denied after the clerks took one look at her.

"I want to buy a gun," Sylvia hissed at the clerk, her nervous twitch, and odd demeanor all too apparent.

"Sorry, we're all out of rifles."

"She didn't put her best face forward at the K-mart store," Orange said. "And the clerks saw her kind before. A nut that wants to buy a gun. They were savvy enough to ask Sylvia the right questions when she kept pressing them. Her mental illness was all too apparent. With that kind of background, she could not legally own a gun."

Sylvia would not be denied, however, as a week later she went to another gun store. She filled out all the forms and lied about the part where they ask if the applicant has ever been mentally ill or had a police record. She then walked out of the store with her long sought after weapon.

"Sylvia was a paranoid schizophrenic but had a high IQ," Orange said. "She went to the Kmart and learned what the clerks would ask for. When she went to the second gun dealership, she didn't make the same mistake twice. She would play it cool and lie about her background."

"Sylvia Seegrist was able to purchase a weapon," Eshleman said. "When she was asked if she had a history of mental illness she simply checked 'no' on the form. She was able to purchase a .22 caliber semi-automatic rifle for a $104 dollars. No problems whatsoever."

SHOOTING UP A MALL

"There were reports of her showing up at the mall days before the shooting," Kanely said. "She was actually marching up and down in front of the doors, in front of stores. "

But it wasn't time yet. Sylvia would wait until her rage reached a point of no return.

That would be the day before Halloween and that might explain why no one noticed Sylvia walking up to the mall wearing camouflage pants, military combat boots, a wool cap and a shirt with the word Jihad emblazoned across the back.

"Remember that this occurred in the mid-1980s," Orange said. "There was plenty of controversy in the aftermath regarding the mentally ill vis a vis gun control. But the fact that Sylvia wore a shirt with Jihad written across the back was a minor detail in those days, to say the least. If her crime had been committed in this day and age, the media would be focused on her supposed radical Islam beliefs just as they were with the San Bernardino shooters."

Earlier in the day, Sylvia had been denied her psychiatric medication at the mall pharmacy because she did not have her welfare card.

"This happens more than you think," Orange said. "A mentally ill patient cannot get their prescription filled for whatever reason. In Sylvia's case, she forgot her medi-caid card. So she is already paranoid and thinks that the world is out to get her. When the pharmacist refuses to give her what she wants, she cannot control her own anger. It feeds into her already strong sense of persecution. Everyone is against her. Everyone is out to get her. The voices in her head build to an irrational rage and she needs a release. A release that has been twenty-five years in the making and now coming to fruition with the purchase of a new rifle. The medication she was on could have dulled her rage, dulled her senses. But now without her drugs the lid was off the coffee pot, so to speak."

"Sylvia was the type of schizophrenic that heard voices," Orange said. "And those voices didn't have her best interests in mind. It was reported numerous times that she was seen talking to herself while marching up and down the shopping mall hallways. Well, she was talking to the voices in her head. Those voices would eventually tell her to buy a gun and shoot the place up. These voices may have been telling her to do what she did for a very long time. She finally listened."

Her rage reaching a boiling point, Sylvia loaded up her .22 caliber semi-automatic rifle and filled her pockets with bullets. She muttered curse words to herself as she drove from her residence in Crum Lynne to Springfield, Pennsylvania.

Her destination, the Springfield Mall.

"The Springfield Mall is a huge place," Orange said. "Back then they had a Bamberger's (now a Macy's store) and over seventy stores spread across a huge lot. It was a favorite hangout out of Sylvia. She knew the ins and outs of that mall."

She parked her white Datsun near the entrance of the mall and began shooting at patrons leaving the shopping center. Her first victim was Edward Seitz, the first person she saw when she stepped out of her vehicle. Sylvia fired two shots at Seitz but missed because he was too far away (thirty yards). The man began to run. Sylvia muttered something incomprehensible to herself then continued on to the mall entrance.

Seitz saw the white Datsun that Sylvia was driving. He had the wherewithal to slash one of Sylvia's tires in the hopes of preventing her escape.

"After him (Seitz) was a woman standing at an automated teller machine," Kanely said. "She was not hit. Initially, witnesses thought they were looking at a male because of the way the person was dressed."

The woman didn't get a good look at Sylvia as she ran away from the ATM machine. She called the police and told them that there was a small man dressed in military fatigues shooting up the mall.

"The scene that day was sort of a mixture of confusion then chaos," Eshleman said. "She was firing indiscriminately. She was firing off her hip. She wasn't aiming at anybody, per se."

Several people were wounded as Sylvia ran inside the mall, firing her rifle as if she were a soldier at war...a soldier mumbling to herself.

"Once she came into the mall, it was more chaos," Eshleman said. "She just began firing indiscriminately. They (customers) were diving behind racks of clothing. They were running behind the rear of stores."

"It appeared that she didn't take notice of any characteristics of people in deciding whether they were going to be shot at or not," Kanely said. "She just shot."

She would kill two-year-old Recife Cosmen who was entering a Magic Pan restaurant with his parents. The boy died instantly while two other children, Recife's cousins, ten-year-old Tiffany Wootson and nine-year-old Kareen Wootson were hit but would survive.

"The .22 caliber bullet is a relatively small one," Orange said. "But the effect on a child's body is catastrophic. The young boy was shot in the chest. He would die from massive internal bleeding."

"At the time I was a young father with young children," Eshleman said. "And looking back on that I think 'It could have been us.' I mean I think that's when it sort of hits you."

Sylvia showed no remorse as the mother of her victim wailed in grief. She was a woman on a mission and walked further into the mall.

Firing at will. She ignored some stores. Others she shot up.

"People at first were not sure what was going on," reporter Russell Eshleman said. "This was the day before Halloween. Mischief night. So a number of people that it was some sort of Halloween prank. Someone in a costume who was pretending to be a killer."

Sylvia shot up store windows and random people, cursing aloud and grinding her teeth.

"It is the sort of crime that hits people right where their fears are," journalist Reid Kanaley said. "Nothing is going to happen to me while I'm out shopping. This one stood out because it occurred in a public place and it was perpetrated by a woman."

Sylvia continued to shoot people at random, more minutes passed. More screaming and chaos.

Elderly Ernest Trout stepped out of a store and walked directly in front of Sylvia.

"He didn't realize what was going on," Orange said. "He didn't know that the place was being shot up. He was deep in thought, looking at his purchase. When he looked up, he saw Sylvia standing in front of him with her rifle aimed at his chest."

The schizophrenic didn't hesitate, firing at the senior citizen three times. Trout, a retired physician, would later die from bullet wounds to his head and stomach.

"I don't think she was picking on senior citizens at the time," Eshleman said. "I think it just happened to be people who got in the way of her bullets."

The next victim would be sixty-four-year-old August Ferrara. Like Trout, Ferrara would step out of a store and stand directly in Sylvia's line of fire. He would die on the shopping mall floor.

Sylvia showed no signs of slowing down as she carried her rifle throughout the shopping center. The voices in her head told her to keep going.

Keep shooting. You have plenty of bullets.

Sylvia sprinted toward Kinney's Shoes, firing her weapon when she confronted by John Laufler, who came out of the store in a fit of anger. Laufler, a twenty-four-year-old grad student, thought Sylvia was pulling a Halloween prank that had gone too far.

"The hell are you doing?" Laufler said, grabbing the rifle out of Sylvia's hand.

The paranoid schizophrenic just looked up at the young man, staring.

"The hell are you doing? You messed with the wrong dude. I don't know what the hell you're doing but I'm calling security? You hear me?"

Sylvia did nothing but nod her head.

"You picked the wrong person to mess with," Laufler said. "I'm turning you in."

"I'm a woman," Sylvia pleaded. "And I have seizures."

Laufler did not know that the bullets Sylvia had fired were real.

"I just felt that she was causing such a panic, even if it was a prank, it was a bad prank," Laufer said.

"When Laufler stopped her, he broke her out of her delusion," Orange said. "She snapped out of it, so to speak. What he said to her brought her back to reality, however brief. Brief enough for her to put the gun down and stop shooting."

Sylvia sat obediently in the store as Laufler came back with a security guard.

"Why?" the security guard asked. "Why did you do it?"

"My family makes me nervous," Sylvia said as she was handcuffed and forced to wait for the police.

"You killed people."

"I didn't mean to do it," Sylvia mumbled. "I didn't mean to do it. I didn't mean to do it."

The voices no longer screaming in her head, Sylvia would remain calm as the police arrived and took her to jail.

The rampage was one of the first to start the debate of mental illness and its treatment as well as the ability for such a person to purchase firearms.

TRIAL

Sylvia was led into the courtroom by one burly deputy and a female sheriff. They sat her at the defendant's table as the judge prepared his opening remarks. He read off the charges against her then looked the paranoid schizophrenic in the eye.

"Do you understand the charges against you?" the judge asked.

"Fuck you," Sylvia said. "I hope you starve, mother fucker. I don't like that feeling, but that's the way it is."

Sylvia would be charged with three counts of first-degree murder and seven counts of attempted murder. Her psychotic behavior continued at her trial as she stood before Judge Joseph DiPietro.

"Hurry up, man!" Sylvia shouted up at the judge. "You know I'm guilty. Kill me on the spot."

Psychiatrists, however, would intervene and declare Sylvia unfit to stand trial. She would be returned to the mental institution for six months. After further evaluation, Sylvia was then judged competent enough to stand trial.

On June 27th, 1986, she would be convicted of all the counts levied against but would also be declared mentally ill. Sylvia would be sentenced to three consecutive terms of life imprisonment.

Her attorneys continued to press for the prospect of Sylvia returning to society if she showed improvement in therapy but her trial judge nixed the idea immediately.

"She should not be back on the street," Judge Robert Kelly said, noting that Pennsylvania has very strict laws that prevent prisoners convicted of homicide to go back on the street even if they were declared mentally ill.

Sylvia herself would take it upon herself to write politicians in her area and implore them to have stricter gun control laws.

"She wrote senators then President Clinton," Kanely said. "In letters sometimes describing what she had done and saying 'I shouldn't have been allowed to get this gun.'"

Sylvia remains in a Pennsylvania state prison.

THE ORLANDO SHOOTER

ALICE WILLIS-WILDER

The Orlando Shootings left behind them a trail of mental and emotional devastation for a nation already so divided. On the 16th of June of 2016, Omar Mateen, a young American man walked into a gay nightclub named Pulse in Orlando, where he opened fire on the crowd. Forty-nine people lost their lives and fifty-three more were injured. In the aftermath, Mateen was shot by law enforcement as he refused to give himself in or hand over his weapon over a three hour standoff.

This event was painful for America, as well as for many other inhabitants of First World Nations and people across the Islamic world. So many people and circumstances and identities were involved in the situation, that for many it was hard to make sense of what had just happened. The deadliest mass shooting by a single shooter in all of US history, not to mention the deadliest single act of violence against the LGBT community had just taken place. Yet it was uncertain at first what had motivated the attack in the first place. The public waited with baited breath as debates ran on whether the source of the attack was homophobia, whether the attack was completely random, or whether it was something else. Then, as evidence emerged that Omar Mateen had stated that his actions were due to the current and historical United States interventions and campaigns in the Arabic-speaking, Islamic world, a new wave of suspicion arose. Press releases began questioning whether Mateen acted out of religious hatred, whether he targeted a homosexual nightclub specifically or whether it was a random target, whether he had any association to any known terrorist organizations or whether he acted alone. Mateen was also an Arab-American and his victims were primarily Hispanic, causing suggestions of racial tension to arise. Furthermore with Mateen being a security guard and his victims being minorities, as well as the fact that he, a minority himself, was killed by police, the public once more questioned the role of law enforcement in the unlawful deaths of minorities across the United States. In a nation with so much conflict between its citizens, the Orlando Shootings represented the start of a stronger divide. Fear and distrust became more widespread in the few days following the incident, with every new piece of information causing the public to voice their concern over the state of the United States. Homosexuals felt concerned about their safety and the security of their favorite social areas. Muslims felt targeted and threatened by a media that sought to make the connection between Mateen's actions and his faith. Minorities worried more than ever about the gun violence perpetrated against them and the role of law enforcement in their unnatural deaths. Anti-war activists worried that their causes would be detracted from by Mateen's statements and association. Veterans, soldiers, and police worried that they may be the targets of vengeful violence. Nobody was safe.

In order to construct a stronger, better image of the events that took place in the early hours of that morning, it is necessary to build a better, fairer, more human image of Omar Mateen. The panic and anger caused by sensationalist media who would seize and spin any tiny piece of information into a full speculative story has driven the United States to division. But the reality, although less comfortable or easy to pick apart, may bring together a country where, at present, fear and distrust has forced wedges between us all.

Mateen was born on the 16th of November 1986 to Afghan immigrant parents in New York. His parents moved to the United States in the 1980s and were keen to live the American dream. Although Muslims, his family were as moderate as can be without being truly secular and embraced American values. They aimed to be an all-American family and raised their son as a proper citizen. However despite his moderate upbringing, Mateen had a troubled mind that was evident from a young age. By the time he joined elementary school they had moved to Port St. Lucie. There he enrolled in Mariposa Elementary, where he attended regular classes. By third grade, his deviant behavior had already begun to take hold. From unknown influences, Mateen had developed a knowledge about sex and violence, both of which he was developing a fascination with. His teacher wrote in his report that he was a very active child who was constantly moving. However unlike some healthily energetic children, Mateen's focus was different. He was "verbally abusive, rude and aggressive" to the other students, using explicit language related to sex and violence. He would not respect the personal boundaries of the other children, grabbing and touching them despite protests. Although these issues were identified so young, they were left unaddressed, assumed to be a phase or generally written off as incidental. His father, who despite moderateness still retained some cultural influences from the more misogynistic Afghani environment he was raised in, had little time for Mateen's female teachers. When they presented complaints about his son, his father was suspicious of their reasoning. And considering the way that his high energy was often lumped in with violence in his reports, it is possible that the school did itself a disservice, presenting an image which, to a less involved parent who did not witness the incidents, may simply sound like an overreaction to the natural behaviour of a young child. Thus, Mateen's issues were underexamined, belittled and repressed. No corrections would have happened at home and the school's only leverage, as is the case for many educational facilities, consisted solely of punishment without parental involvement. In essence, Mateen was left to handle his troubles on his own.

The result of this neglect was a snowball. By seventh grade, Mateen was moved out of regular schooling and into a special, separate class, due to increased conflict between him and other students. But it was too little too late. Rather than help him, his school merely confined and punished him. And after years of becoming increasingly violent and behaviorally abnormal, Mateen only continued to worsen. His grades plummeted further due to his behavioral problems, incidences of conflict and attempts at correction, all of which disturbed his schooling. Bullying was reported from both sides for Mateen. Some of his classmates found him to be an insufferable bully who acted like he was better than his peers, disrespected girls and hurt other children, threatening to start conflict. Others saw him being bullied himself, for his ethnic heritage, his religion, his weight and other issues. It was clear that Mateen did not feel like he belonged there and did not know how to fit in at school. However, the behavior continued to worsen, unaddressed and dismissed, with the rift between his parents and his teachers constantly growing.

His elementary school teachers, without the cooperation of his parents, were not able to set Mateen on the right track. And their concerns were more than valid. Entering Martin County high school in the year 2000, Mateen's anger and fixation on violence continued to spiral out of control. Beyond threats and inappropriately touching other students, he began to get physically involved in his aggressive outbursts. At the age of fourteen, he became involved in a fight during math class and the physical aggression meant that the police had to be involved. Mateen was arrested and charged with battery and disrupting the safe educational environment of the school. The school later thought it in Mateen's best interests for the charges to be dropped, assuming a lesson had been learned, although he was expelled. A dean at Martin County high school notes that various efforts were made to counsel him and redirect his violence. But Mateen seemed blind to the errors of his ways, instead developing pride in his ability to hurt and offend others. As he continued to hide his disorderly behavior from his father, Mateen had become an uncorrectable student for Martin County high school, with his father continually taking his side and teachers unable to break through his psychopathic fixations. He could not be reintegrated. Mateen was instead moved to Spectrum, a local high school which adopted alternative educational methods to correct students whose behavior was considered seriously maladaptive or dangerous to themselves and others. However, even there Mateen stood out for his troubling behavior. Despite his moderate upbringing, his thirst for violence had already driven him to voice his support for terrorist groups. And, without any American friends to guide him towards more constructive outlets for his energy, this support was allowed to grow inside him. He did not trust his parents with the issues he was suffering, possibly so that they would not punish him, he pushed teachers away violently and alienated peers who may have become good influences on his life. Instead, he became increasingly absorbed in himself and his own fascination with violence and Islamic terrorism. Mateen had named Osama bin Laden, a minor terrorist at the time, but known nonetheless, as his uncle, and claimed that Osama had taught him how to shoot AK-47s. This insight suggests that Mateen was learning about terrorism and terrorist figures from somewhere. Although his teenage story was far-fetched, it seems likely that the seeds of his claims were planted by another influence, one that garnered more respect than other teenagers, but was less scary to the young boy than his parents' discipline. In the wake of the September 11 attacks, Mateen cheered for the hijackers and continued to voice his support for terrorist action. Due to the traumatic nature of the attacks on American citizens, the teachers and students at Spectrum included, and Mateen's insensitive and disturbing behavior, his father was called to pick him up. No longer able to deny that his son was behaving in a way that was threatening to other students, disruptive to school and casting a bad light on their faith and ethnicity, Mateen's father was overcome with rage. He slapped Mateen in the face as he collected him. Mateen was suspended from school for five days after the incident.

From this point, Mateen had yet another item in his arsenal of offensive and violent imagery. Realizing the shock this caused the other students at Spectrum, Mateen began to imitate the sounds of an exploding plane whilst on the school bus, causing disruption, and continued to voice support for the attacks and for Osama. Mateen seemed oblivious to the mood and state of mind of the other students, instead becoming excited at anything that could be considered taboo: drugs, sex, violence and terrorism all fascinated and revitalized him.

After yet another fight, Mateen was sent to another school, this time, St Lucie West Centennial high school. During his stay at high school, Mateen's violent nature had developed out of control. Over his years at various schools, he had accumulated forty-eight days of suspensions for his involvement in fights and the injuries he had caused other students. Around the same time, his father had been becoming more and more unstable behind the scenes. Although Mateen's family was more American than Afghani, the Afghanistan war weighed heavily on his more traditional father, who felt torn between his birth country and his adoptive homeland. Despite not being particularly religiously conservative, Mr. Mateen began to engage politically, to a point of delusion, posting videos of himself in uniform as he pretended to be the president of Afghanistan for a bemused social media. But for the family, it was no laughing matter. They already encountered divisiveness at school and in the neighborhood due to the American press's aggressively patriotic propaganda against Afghanistan, their home country. And Mr. Mateen's behavior only brought about further divides. Mateen's sisters began to say they were Persian, to avoid accusations of Islamic extremism. But Mateen's own concept of shame and sense of self seemed different to his mother and sisters, instead he was closer to what his father was like. He would gladly not only defend his homeland but the very terrorists he was being associated with and seek to get a rise out of other students however he could, for his entire childhood. That his father himself appeared to be suffering mental health issues may go some way to explaining why Mateen's behavior was not addressed. Nothing wrong was seen by his father, so nothing was punished.

Mateen appeared to calm some of this behavior as he began to apply for college. At first, it seemed as though leaving the pressurized high school environment that had stressed him and brought him into bullying situations had worked. It seemed to all who could see him that he was a changed young man, refocused on his life and career, eager to escape the mess he had made in his childhood. However, even then there were small signs that his reformation was not at all complete. Mateen enrolled in Indian River State College and applied for their Criminal Justice Training program. As part of his applications questionnaire he had to state whether he had committed any crimes, known or unknown. Although he stated in the questionnaire that he had committed or been involved in a crime that went undetected, he provided no specific details and inquiries were not made. Mateen followed his education with focus, to all appearances casting off his violent and sadistic nature in favor of his degree. He took on several jobs, laid low, was not hostile towards members of the faculty and generally focused on his studies. It looked as though he had completely grown out of his teenage violence. He remained a highly private person and rather than focus on his obsessions, he developed new ones. Mateen began to focus on his physical appearance and health, retreating into the gym, his diet, and a new habit of steroids. This focus, combined with his previous teenage love for soccer and skateboarding, allowed him to lose the fat that he had been bullied for most of his childhood and develop a physique that pleased him most of the time. Despite his steroid use and unstable mental health, Mateen's privacy managed to keep him out of trouble for the duration of his course. In 2006, he graduated with an associate of science degree in Criminal Justice Technology. This degree would be his gateway to weapons, training and the sort of status which would later allow him to get away with murder... or at least with plotting it.

After graduating, Mateen changed his surname, originally Omar Mir Seddique, to Omar Mir Seddique Mateen, matching his surname to his parents. He also registered to vote as a member of the Democratic Party. In all, he did throughout college and in that final year, Mateen was showing himself off as a normal, empathic, responsible citizen. It is uncertain whether his actions were intentionally disarming and intended to more easily place him in a position of power and responsibility, or whether he was acting impulsively and seeking validation in all he did. However, every step he took appeared calculated to make him seem small, gentle, kind, a family man, and generally a trustworthy American citizen. A few months after obtaining his degree, he immediately began working as a recruit for the Florida Department of Corrections, where he was assigned to the Martin Correctional Institution. During this application, the standards for past criminal activity were tighter than for college, and Mateen had to declare his full criminal history. However, all he had to mention were his arrest at school when he was fourteen and experimentation with marijuana. In the eyes of the law, Mateen was a kid who had fallen off the path, seen the error of his ways and completely turned around. His interest in justice and defense was rational, given his history, and his improvements over his college years were undeniable. However, in a situation where violence was more common and where he was once more forced to work with others, it didn't take long for Mateen's dangerous mind to become evident once more. At a time when concerns were heightened due to the shooting at Virginia Tech in 2007, Mateen was not able to hide his unusual obsession much longer. He openly inquired in class whether he would tell anyone if he chose to bring a gun to class with him. This suggestion raised the concern of his warden, who wrote in a report that the inappropriateness in the timing of the remark seemed disturbing at best, and very bad sign at worst. A few days after the report was written Mateen was dismissed from the program, never attaining certification as a corrections officer.

However, he was determined to continue his security work, despite being consistently deemed unfit for it. He gained a concealed carry permit and an armed security guard license, passing the psychological and physical tests required. However, the doctor administering the tests was Dr. Syed Shefeeq Rahman, who had close ties with Mateen's family. This may have had some influence on his next employer's hiring of him. G4S Secure Solutions, a British security firm which handled such events as the London 2012 Olympics, hired Mateen in 2007. However, since the Olympics, it has emerged that their hiring practices were less than adequate and their background searches less than rigorous. Between a possibly falsified health report and G4S's lax testing standards, Mateen passed two security screenings, one in 2007 and another in 2013, which allowed him to work for G4S as an armed guard for them. This is not only despite his own criminal history but also despite his continued comments about terrorism. Mateen did not alter his behavior when working for G4S, however, they did not see it fit to fire him and his comments about terrorist acts and supporting terrorists did not raise any red flags in his screenings. That said, G4S were well aware of Mateen's behavior, as he was initially put in a role at a courthouse, from which he had to be removed due to his remarks that suggested he had been involved in terrorist acts. Once more, where alarm bells should have rung, Mateen's peers and superiors wrote his behavior off as eccentricity, moving him to a small kiosk in a gated community. Unaddressed and uncorrected, Mateen's attitude continued to worsen. He developed a stronger and stronger cynical streak, observing the altruism and hard work of people after disasters and stating that he believed humans waited for such events and longed to be involved in the clean up so they had work to do.

In 2008 Mateen met an Uzbeki immigrant woman through MySpace and began to show interest in her. On the 16th of April of 2009, they married. However, they separated after mere months and eventually divorced in 2011. His ex-wife, Sitora Yusufiy, described the chaos that was living with Mateen to the press after the Orlando nightclub shooting. Like many who grew to know him, she found he was a quiet, amiable man at first. He "seemed like a normal human being" to her. He was not at all religious but a quiet man, gentle and caring. However as time went by, other facets to his personality were revealed to her. Despite not being religious, Mateen glorified extreme Islamic practices usually only seen under Sharia law. He also displayed mental instability, and it was eventually revealed to her that he suffered from bipolar disorder. His everyday life was a constant crisis of identity. On the one hand, Mateen adored and admired terrorists, desired an extremely traditional Islamic household and was an aggressive and unstable man with a mental disorder and a history of taking steroids. On the other hand, he was not even remotely a follower of Islam, desired to be a normal American citizen and held it as his goal to become a law enforcement officer, preferably a policeman. After a few months together Mateen began to beat Yusufiy. His temper was short and he identified himself largely by what he hated, rather than what he loved or aspired to. Much like his own father seemed to have done in his own life, Mateen used no other outlet for these angry emotions but violence. He owned a gun, isolated Yusufiy from her family and regularly physically assaulted her. Eventually, after a few months, her family had enough of the situation and helped Yusufiy to escape. The divorce was not final until two years later.

By the next year, he had married again, this time to Noor Salman. The desperate way in which he sought female attention in the interim suggested a man who was unstable, nervous, seeking validation or guidance, something to fill a void in his life. He went through usernames like wildfire, which normally suggests that a certain stigma became attached to previous usernames. It was clear that his odd behavior extended beyond his teenage years and interactions in person. Even online, where it is generally easier to create a better impression of yourself, Mateen had difficulty identifying and matching the mood of those he spoke to. He would also lie about his age and begin stalking particular women, using his new usernames to monitor them even after being blocked, messaging them to say he had found where they lived or worked, that he knew the color of their car... and that he was nearby.

In 2013, after his second security screening which he also passed, Mateen was found to be making inflammatory comments which might have brought danger on himself or his co-workers. At this point he was moved from the G4S security post he had held at the courthouse in his security work at the gated community, where such claims were harder to make. Never focused on religion and instead on violence and terrorism, Mateen would routinely make claims to belong to different opposing Islamic extremist terrorist factions, from the Sunni Al Qaeda, to the Shiite Hezbollah. Despite these claims being outlandish and generally focused on whichever terrorist group garnered the most attention, the comments were taken seriously enough that the local county sheriff's office wrote to the Federal Bureau of Investigation. An investigation began into Mateen, but due to the randomness and weakness of his claims, as well as how they changed and the complete lack of evidence, the Federal Bureau of Investigation closed the inquiry as inconclusive. But it took less than a year for Mateen to capture their attention again. He had been known to talk to an individual at his local mosque, the Islamic Center of Fort Pierce, who later returned to Syria to carry out a suicide bombing. With Mateen's history and possible association, the old inquiry was reopened and investigated. However, the federal investigators on the case once more found that Mateen had no visible ties to terrorism and noted that his relationship with the bomber was more one of a casual acquaintance.

The mosque itself noted that although he attended, there was nothing to suggest his faith was particularly strong or radicalized. Their teachings were of peace and survival for a harsh world where their community may face discrimination, and Mateen himself remained a passive member of the mosque, attending prayer and then going back home. Despite consistently claiming to belong to Islamic terrorist organizations, his own Islamic ties were weak and his faith seemed like yet another attempt to appear to be an upstanding member of the community. But the opposite was very much true. Even in his lower contact role, Mateen was hostile to those he worked with and sought to distinguish himself and elevate himself above them. He was on edge, constantly concerned that someone had insulted him. However, he would never discuss these apparent insults, instead releasing the energy physically, slamming objects and doors until the rage passed. If he felt he had been disrespected he would engage in passive-aggressive behavior, making people wait at the gate, causing queues and delays. He would also use his prayers as an excuse when he needed to, so as to further delay those who had offended him. He displayed tension and aggression when dealing with the residents, grabbing their ID, glaring at them, getting close to their faces with a menacing or tense expression, with the muscles in his jaw and neck visible. However when confronted about this behavior once more he would adopt a passive attitude, avoiding displaying emotion or engaging other angry people. He would blankly stare and wait for the incident to be over. After a serious confrontation he would treat that resident more respectfully, but always cold and detached.

It had been abundantly clear, throughout Mateen's life, that he was an unstable individual. He had a fixation on violence and terrorism from a very young age, which had led him to violent and criminal behavior in turn. His family, like many immigrant families from strongly traditional backgrounds, were alternately dismissive of his troubles and harsh in their punishment of him. However with Mateen, this meant more than exclusion from his peers and uncomfortable family meetings as an adult. Mateen was not a normal individual, and his fixation on violence, cynicism towards human nature and eagerness to hurt and offend others marked out the perfect profile of a psychopath. A lifetime of bullying and educational neglect had left him with little affection for his mentors or his peers, and his obsession with terrorism and working in a security and defense role put him in a position where his lust for violence was fed and his access to weapons guaranteed. A person in Mateen's position should never have been left free in the community, let alone placed in a position to protect and guard the very civilians he longed to harm.

Omar Mateen was developing a serious rage against society. Although the target of the attack was a gay nightclub and although he repeatedly claimed ties to Islamic extremism, from his history it is clearer that the attacks came from a place of personal rage. Mateen believed society and life had short changed him. The young boy who had worked so hard to lose weight, to correct his attitude, to find a wife and to become a police officer was a disrespected, insecure security guard at a small gated community. Despite his FBI investigations, being rejected by law enforcement, his history of domestic violence and being mentally unstable, he still held his concealed carry permit and an armed security license. Despite this, his first attempts to get armed for the incident were foiled. Mere weeks before the shooting, Mateen walked into Lotus Gunworks and started asking for heavy-duty body armor, exactly like that used by riot police. The owner thought the request and phrasing were very odd, but they did not sell body armor anyway and explained this to him. Immediately afterward Mateen asked to buy bulk ammunition. The questions he was asking were also highly suspicious, not at all the normal questions of a gun fanatic, hunter or reenactment actor. Furthermore, Mateen spent some time talking on the phone in a Middle Eastern tongue which the staff correctly or mistakenly identified as Arabic, and walking around the store texting, rather than engaging with the staff. The two requests and his attitude set off alarm bells and the store refused to sell Mateen anything at all, reporting him to the Federal Bureau of Investigation immediately after the incident. The FBI withheld their commentary on the incident.

However, Lotus Gunworks's more careful and measured approach was not held by everyone. Either Mateen managed to mask his lifelong awkward and insensitive behavior, or someone was out to make a quick sale because a few days later Mateen walked into the St Lucie Shooting Center and placed his order for the weapons he would use in the attack. He passed the necessary background checks and nothing was noted as being amiss by staff or owner this time. Under Florida law, he was allowed to own a long gun like an AR-15 without even having a license, but his armed security qualifications and concealed carry permit placed him in a position where this law was irrelevant. Days before the attack, Mateen had the weapons in his hands. A Sig Sauer MCX and a semi-automatic pistol. The former seemed almost inspired by previous terrorist acts, as the Colorado movie theater massacre, the Sandy Hook massacre and the San Bernadino massacre all involved long guns. The Sig Sauer MCX was bought with a simple background check, without the need of his license and the handgun had been approved for concealed carry. After the stopping of a motion which would have prevented people on the FBI watch list from buying guns, Mateen was in a secure place. Even if he had been on the FBI watch lists, the absence of checks at earlier stages, such as his concealed carry permit, and the lack of reports for his violent outbursts, meant that there would have been nothing to stop him buying them regardless.

On the 11th of June, when the attack began, the nightclub was hosting its Latin Night, a Saturday night event especially for the local Hispanic LGBT community. The night was getting quiet around 2am on the morning of the 12th, with only 320 people left inside for their last round of drinks. Omar Mateen had chosen an interesting time to strike, however, it is unclear whether this was intentional or whether he simply began as the mood struck him in the midst of an episode. He drove down to the club in his van, parking on the road and covering the small distance to the club door by foot, carrying his long gun and handgun in the dark to the door. A security guard, an off-duty uniformed Orlando Police Department Officer, engaged Mateen. However, Mateen somehow gained access, where he immediately began shooting the people inside the club. Two additional officers stepped in to stop him, but he retreated deep into the nightclub where he took several hostages. At that time of the night and with such short notice, it took 45 minutes for a hundred officers from the Orlando Police Department to arrive at the scene. Mateen's attack was haphazard and not targeted at any individuals. As such, despite being trapped, the patrons were able to call or send text messages to their loved ones. At first, some who had not witnessed Mateen's entrance assumed the gunshots were firecrackers or a theme in the music. As the music continued to play and the lights remained low, Mateen advanced through the unsuspecting crowd with ease, taking several hostages to ward off the security guards. From his training, he knew that if he were able to get even one hostage, the security guards would not be able to move in on him. Mateen opened fire again inside the club. A bartender hid behind the glass bar. Unharmed patrons attempted to help those who had been shot.

With the arrival of the police imminent, Mateen retreated towards the bathrooms, finding several people hiding there. He opened fire inside the confined space. His hostage attempted to escape and was injured by two bullets and by pieces of the damaged wall which crumbled onto them. Mateen's rifle jammed before he could kill them all, but he maintained his composure and took the survivors hostage. They were unaware that his weapon had been temporarily disabled and quietly followed him, as the shooter remarked about not having anything against other minorities and that he would not stop attacking until the United States stopped bombing his country. As the panic progressed, Mateen claimed he had explosives and several snipers supporting him from outside the club, causing patrons to call and text 911 to try and alert police of these claims. But this was all his own panic as Mateen realized that he was stuck in the club, alone, with a jammed weapon and police waiting for him outside. At twenty-two minutes past two, not even half an hour into the attack, Mateen himself called the police. He began rambling over the phone call, mentioning previous terrorist attacks and how they had inspired him. From Tamerlan and Dzhokhar Tsarnaev to Moner Mohammad Abu Salha, Mateen expressed his appreciation for their works and how he had been motivated by their dedication to swear allegiance to ISIL.

Although the calls were short, Mateen made two more during the course of the shooting, each time referencing previous terrorist acts and his own supposed membership to ISIL.

With the situation reaching beyond crisis point, there was an exchange of gunfire between Mateen and the security guard, after which police officers began to floor in through a glass window. However, they were not properly prepared for the weapons Mateen was handling. They were told to track Mateen and wait until the SWAT team arrived in tactical gear. They tracked him back to the bathroom area and after fifteen or twenty minutes the SWAT team took over the operation. By this point, all the security forces that would be present had assembled and there was tension in the air as Mateen's claim he was carrying a bomb became a pressing concern. At this point, Mateen called the police again, identified himself as the shooter at Pulse nightclub and explained that he was doing this attack on behalf of ISIL, at which point he began speaking in Arabic for the remainder of the call. A crisis negotiator was present and hostage negotiators also began to speak with Mateen by telephone, through the number supplied by the police. Mateen refused to cooperate, acting defiantly. He also claimed again to have bombs strapped to his body.

It was not until almost four in the morning that the Orlando Police Department released a public statement that there was a shooting ongoing at Pulse nightclub and that there were multiple injuries. Hardly half an hour afterward, Mateen scaled his claims. He stated that he was strapping explosive vests to four hostages, placing them at the corners of the building and detonating them within fifteen minutes. This claim triggered the response of the Orlando Police Department Officers, who ended negotiations and charged into the building to prevent the possible explosion. Between the break in of first responders and this breaching of the wall no gunshots had been heard. The SWAT team initially attempted to enter the building by detonating a bomb, but this failed to cause an opening. As he realized that his time was running out, Mateen entered the bathroom stall where the hostages were hiding and fired at them, killing one of them. At five in the morning, the SWAT officers breached the building by driving an armored vehicle through a wall. They used flashbangs to distract Mateen as they entered, but a shootout began between him and eleven officers and Mateen was killed. The building was evacuated and thirty hostages were freed. No further guns or explosives were found.

Although the horrific incident left the nation in pain and afraid, it is clear from Mateen's background that these were not the plans of a sophisticated terrorist organization. Nor were his motivations clear. Although he claimed the attacks were related to the bombing of the Middle East, his idolization of terrorists extended beyond the glory a young man holds for his heroes. He valued them for their terrorist actions, not for their faith or their missions. His choice of attack venue may have reflected his own perspective of what Islam ought to be, however considering he was a regular patron, it is just as likely that he simply chose a venue he was familiar with. And choosing to attack the club on Hispanic night appears to have had less to do with their race and more to do with his own impulses. Omar Mateen might have been a Muslim, he might have been a homophobe, he might have been bisexual and he might have been racist. However, none of this emerges from the picture of his past. Rather, the Omar Mateen that existed before the shooting was a paranoid, bipolar, psychopathic young man, a young man who resented the world for everything it denied him, a young man who was afraid of being ignored or disrespected, a young man who lived to shock and horrify others just to be noticed. This was not a crime of faith or of passion or of political activism.

This was, like almost every other mass shooting in the USA, a crime of insanity.

A SERIAL KILLER'S ROAD TRIP

Nathan Nixon

Charles Starkweather

The 1950's for the United States of America is best remembered as some of the most trying times in the history of the nation. While the early 1950's saw the baby boom, the late half of the decade was marred by civil instability and mistrust. Many Americans, especially those in the southern United States, lost their trust in the American dream as well as the government. Many of those Americans took their destiny into their own hands.

Charles Starkweather may have been the epitome of the decline of human morals in the late 1950's. In one of the most notable murder sprees in the modern era, Hollywood has recreated the life of Charles Starkweather many times over.

Charles Starkweather is best known for a murder spree that spanned over the course of just a few months. The circumstances surrounding this reign of terror make it unique to the crime community.

Charles Raymond "Charlie" Starkweather was born on November 24, 1938 in the rural city of Lincoln, Nebraska. As was common in the earlier eras of the 20th century, Starkweather was a part of a large family. He was the third of seven siblings to be born. While he was not especially close to his siblings, he shared a normal relationship with each of them with all factors considered.

Guy Starkweather was Charles' father. Guy fit in with most any southern male at the time. He was a hard-working southern man who took great pride in supporting his family the best that he could. Just after Charles was born, the United States entered into World War II. Due to severe rheumatoid arthritis, Guy was not able to serve his country in the war. While many young children were losing their fathers to the war effort in this era, Charles was lucky enough to have his father at home. Also due to Guy's severe rheumatoid arthritis, he was often unable to complete his work as a carpenter. When Guy was not having a medical flare up of his arthritis, he was well-known in the community as a great wood worker who could complete seemingly any task. However, Guy's condition ultimately led to the Starkweather family living a poor life financially, even by rural standards.

Charles' mother was named Helen Starkweather. Helen was the picture of what a mother should be. She went out of her way to stay active and involved in each of her children's lives. When Guy Starkweather would suffer a flare up and be left unable to work, she would supplement the household income by waitressing. Helen was able to balance this work along with her work at home with taking care of seven children. Helen and Charles shared a good relationship, although he would later admit that he felt "forgotten" as he grew in to his teenage years with so many younger siblings in the house.

Overall, Charles held great memories of his childhood. Unlike most of the killers in the 20th century, he had a strong relationship with his family. Beyond a financially poor situation for most of his childhood, the love and family bond in the home was a great situation for a child to be around.

Charles Starkweather did not share the same happy memories of his education as he did of his family life. He was one of those students who changed drastically from his elementary and middle school years to his high school years. The change was most drastic on his classmates, who could quickly see that Charles was hiding anger from his early years.

A look into the elementary and middle school years of Charles reveals much to behold on some sort of explanation as to why he would carry such a burden. Charles notable had a severe speech impediment. His parents were well aware, even in his toddler years, that his speech was quite different than the rest of his siblings. Financial burdens prevented any sort of speech therapy that could help Charles work through his problem. Throughout his elementary and middle school years, he was bullied nearly every day by his classmates. He would find himself at the center of mean jokes. It was strongly due to this fact that Charles struggled socially at an early age. Many of the other students came after him for being different.

Charles' speech impediment was not the only difference he shared with most of his other classmates. Charles also was born with a condition called genu varum. Genu varum is a birth defect that causes legs to be misshapen in a variety of ways. While individuals with this condition learn to cope and eventually even out as they develop more fully, it was yet another source of bullying that Charles endured. With a speech impediment and a birth defect that affected the look of his legs, Charles Starkweather endured treatment from his classmates that no child should have to endure. Even at a young age, Charles learned quickly that people could be mean.

Even through the bullying in his younger years, Charles Starkweather surprisingly showed no signs of lashing out at his classmates. He more or less took the bullying in stride. While he had very few friends and companions outside of his family, he was an alarmingly quiet child at school.

As Charles entered into his late middle school years, a change became evident in Charles. Charles attended Irving Junior High. It is here that many stories of Charles begin in an attempt to explain a possible motive for his actions. Educationally, Charles struggled tremendously in school. He had a hard time staying focused in many of his core subject classes. Upon beginning his junior high years at Irving, his school problems began to grow. There was one subject, however, that Charles excelled at. Starkweather blossomed in physical education.

Like most other boys his age, Charles was beginning to see his body change. The changes in his body, however, were much more rapid and noticeable than most of his other classmates. Charles was among the tallest and most impressive bodied students in the entire school. The once quiet student who endured more than his fair share of bullies in his elementary years now discovered something. He was bigger than everyone else.

That quiet student who had few friends was not the scared, unassuming boy that many of his teachers and classmates felt that he was. In reality, Charles took note of each student who had bullied him growing up. That is not to say that he had a "list" or anything along those lines. However, he knew that how he was being treated wasn't right. More importantly, he knew that he didn't like it.

Charles Starkweather took gym class as a time to 'get back' at all of those students who had treated him so poorly in his younger years. He would frequently get in fights and make fun of students around him. It took no time at all for Charles' reputation to change. Once considered one of the nicest, most well-behaved students in the school district, he was now considered the "bad child" who didn't fear consequence. Apart from a small circle of friends he gained in junior high and high school, many of the students feared Charles. Most of the students did their best to avoid him at all cost. Bob von Busch, one of his select few friends from his childhood, best sums up the change that everyone noticed in Charles.

"He could be the kindest person you have ever seen. He would actually do anything for you if he found a way to like you. He was a hell of a lot of fun to be around, too. Everything was just one big joke to him. His actions would bring that attitude out in the small group of friends he surrounded himself with. But, he had this other side. A darker side. He could be mean as hell. Just downright cruel. If he saw some poor guy on the street who was bigger than he was, maybe better looking than he was, or better dressed, he would try to take the poor bastard down to his size."

With the change in the personality of Charles Starkweather, it was only a matter of time for more changes to happen. It wouldn't be until Charles turned 17 that the next major change would happen for Charles.

When Charles entered his senior year at 17 years old, his reputation had not changed. While he had a strong circle of friends with whom he had, arguably, too much fun with, he still had the same issues that he previously possessed. He struggled mightily in school, notably lacking any sort of motivation in his studies. Charles didn't do well with authority, either. For this and several other reasons, he would drop out of school just one year short of graduating. He would go on to get his first real job at a Western Union newspaper warehouse. While it didn't pay much money, it offered Charles a chance to get out of the school environment that he hated so much.

In 1956, at just 18 years old, Charles Starkweather would meet the person that would change his life forever. The grounds for their meeting is odd in itself. Charles was introduced to a young, 13-year-old girl named Caril Ann Fugate. Charles was dating Caril's older sister at the time of their introduction. Strangely enough, the two became quite close, often confiding in each other with long talks and intimacy. Shortly after, Charles ended his relationship with Caril's sister. Immediately thereafter, Caril Ann Fugate and Charles Starkweather began their relationship.

Charles' job was located right next to the junior high that Caril attended. He would go be with her each and every day after school. He was considered a terrible employee. His employer described Starkweather just after his murder conviction.

"Sometimes you'd have to tell him the same thing two or three times. Even then, he may not do what he was told because he didn't want to be told. Other times, he struggled understanding basic commands. He was by far the dumbest man we had there."

Caril's and Charles' relationship caused major rifts and consequences and both of their families. It was early in 1957 that Starkweather decided to teach Caril how to drive. He allowed her to drive his 1949 Ford. She quickly crashed the car into another vehicle early one morning. The owner of the Ford, however, was not Charles, but his father Guy. Guy agreed to pay the damages with money that he could hardly spare. This was the breaking point for Guy Starkweather. He banished Charles from the family home and ordered him to never return. With dropping out of school, dating a 13-year-old girl, and crashing the family car, Guy had had enough. Charles, greatly angry at the whole situation, agreed to leave.

Caril's family strongly disapproved of her relationship as well. Obviously, it didn't sit well at all with her parents that she was admittedly dating an 18-year-old boy who had a reputation as a trouble maker. Moreover, at just 13 years old, they felt it was entirely inappropriate for her to be with him in any fashion.

Charles' life was now making another major turn. He was hired on as a garbage collector. He would make minimum wage and struggle to get by for the next several months. But this job had a greater impact than what appears on the surface. During the routes, Charles began to form highly nihilistic views. These views basically meant that whatever circumstance he was currently in was how he was destined to live his life. This was an extremely negative view. He had been in poverty his entire life, and seeing his life turn to working a garbage route for minimum wage helped push him to this gloomy outlook.

Also on these routes, Charles began to plan different robberies. He strongly believed that the best way to change his fortune was to 'take what he wanted'. It was during this time that he would form his famous philosophy on life: "Dead people are all on the same level." He would live the rest of his life by this philosophy. He was not at all shy about this fact either. During his trial, he affirmed this philosophy many times. This officially would mark the beginning of a reign of terror.

The story of Charles Starkweather's murder spree is impossible to tell without understanding the relationship between him and Fugate.

To Charles, Caril was his best friend, his partner in crime. She happily went along with whatever he wanted. She readily broke the rules to be with him. He admired that about her. Charles Starkweather always had something to prove. To most of the investigators surrounding the case, Caril likely gave Charles the confidence and motivation to begin his awful streak. Charles was even able to convince Caril to run away with him. While Caril Ann Fugate denies any knowledge of the murders that Charles would commit beforehand, many believe that Charles convinced Caril to murder her whole family. That fact, however, has never officially been proven.

The circumstance that surrounds Charles' first murder is nothing special all things considered. He didn't have ties to the person he murdered. It wasn't a past childhood acquaintance or even someone that he knew. A late November evening would start one of the most notorious murder sprees in recent history.

In the late hours of November 30, 1957, Charles Starkweather entered a service station in his hometown of Lincoln, Nebraska. Starkweather initially intended to buy a stuffed animal as a gift for Caril. However, he wanted to make the purchase on credit. The clerk that evening, Robert Colvert, refused to complete the sale. Charles became enraged as he stormed out of the store. Charles Starkweather would return to the store three times over the next several hours. He made small purchases. Colvert was disturbed at the awkward behavior of Starkweather.

Finally, Charles Starkweather entered the storm carrying a shotgun. An intense struggle ensued over the gun in which Colvert was injured. Starkweather forced Colvert into his car where he drove him to an extremely remote area on the edge of town. Starkweather forced Colvert out of the car, where he robbed him of $100. After another struggle, Starkweather fired a single shot at point blank range into Robert Colvert's head. With this single shot, Charles Starkweather had committed his first murder.

Charles quickly drove back to Caril Ann Fugate. He confessed to her that he had robbed the service station. However, he foolishly denied actually killing Colvert. He professed to Fugate that someone else had killed Colvert.

During the investigation after the murder spree, Fugate admitted that she didn't believe Starkweather. She knew fully that he had, indeed, murdered Colvert. She claimed that she only went along with the story out of fear of Starkweather. Police, however, never believed that she feared Charlie. Their strong suspicion was that the story and potential for what they were to do was a source of excitement for Caril.

During his murder trial, Starkweather made several eerie sentiments regarding this first murder.

"I had transcended my former self. I reached a new plane of existence in which I was outside the law and could commit any crime without guilt or fear of repercussion."

At this point, Caril and Charles knew that it was only a matter of time before word got around that Charles was, indeed, the killer. This first murder would set off a chain of events that were both devastating and, as the timeline will show, extremely fast.

On January 21, 1958, Starkweather hurried off to the home of Caril Fugate. Caril was not home. Fugate's mother and stepfather, Velda and Marion Bartlett, were at the residence. As was known to Charles, they tried everything that they could to separate Charles and Caril. Caril's parents and Charles Starkweather did not get along. When Charles Starkweather began yelling at them and shouting obscenities, they ordered him to leave the premises and to stay away from Caril. Charles, however, had other plans.

Starkweather returned to his car, and came back to the home with the same shotgun from his first murder. He walked right in the front door and shot both Velda and Marion Bartlett at point blank range. Sadly, they would not be the only two people murdered that afternoon.

Also inside the home was the two-year-old daughter of Velda and Marion Bartlett. Little Billie Jean Bartlett was crying relentlessly at the noise and disturbance in the home. Charles Starkweather proceeded to strangle and stab the innocent Billie Jean. Of all the victims of the murder spree, this is by far the most disturbing.

Caril Ann Fugate would arrive at the home less than one hour later. Upon her arrival, Charles and Caril hid the gruesome bodies of Caril's family behind the house. Great debate has long been had as to the circumstance of this murder. While most everyone believes that Caril and Charles agreed to kill her family as a way for her to be able to flee with him, Caril vehemently denied this fact. She claims that she never intended for her family to be murdered, but that she had no choice but to go along with it after Charles murdered them.

Eerily enough, the couple remained in the house until January 27. With the bodies of her family less than 50 feet away, Caril stayed in the home with Charles. It was only after Caril's grandmother became worried that police were notified that something was happening. This spooked Charles and Caril. It was only then did they decide to hit the road.

Fugate and Starkweather entered into his car and fled the home. They intended to leave Lincoln altogether. Many argue that the murder spree was not planned. Based on Charles behavior and mental state as described after his first murder, most think that he was acting on instinct after the Bartlett murders.

The couple fled on January 27, 1958 to Bennet, Nebraska. They drove to a secluded farmhouse of 70-year-old August Meyer. Meyer was a family friend of the Starkweather family. He was a trusted member of the local community that was known for his blue-collar work ethic and his willingness to help anyone. When Caril and Charles arrived at his home, he never gave a second thought to allowing them to enter his home. Upon entering the home, Charles revealed his shotgun. He quickly fired two powerful blast to the head of August Meyer. For no apparent reason, Charles Starkweather also decided to kill Meyer's dog. The 5th victim of the Starkweather murder spree had just been claimed. The couple spent no time at all at the Meyer house. They took a few valuables and quickly fled the area. Several miles outside of Bennet, Starkweather managed to get their car stuck in the mud on the side of a rural dirt road. Two local teenagers, Robert Jensen and Carol King, came upon their car and offered their help to free the car. When they exited the vehicle, Starkweather brandished his shotgun and forced them to back to their car at gun point. He made them drive Caril and himself back into Bennet. They arrived to an abandoned storm shelter. After they had exited the vehicle, Robert Jensen was shot in the back of the head with the shotgun. Charles then attempted to rape Carol King. King fought with everything she had and was able to hold him off. Frustrated by this, Starkweather shot King in the chest with the barrel just inches away from her body.

During the investigation after his arrest, Starkweather admitted to shooting Jensen, but claimed that Fugate was the one to actually shoot King. While this has never been proven, many believe there is merit to this claim. It is often concluded that Fugate was frustrated that Starkweather had tried to rape King. Upon coming upon the struggle, it is claimed that she picked up the shotgun and fired the shot that killed Carol King.

The couple's next move was to return to Lincoln. Upon entering town, they drove straight to one of the richest neighborhoods in the area. It was here that they entered the home of wealthy industrialist C. Lauer Ward. Lauer was not home, however his wife and their maid were. When the couple entered the home, they immediately stabbed Lauer's wife Clara as well as the housekeeper. To add further death to the scene, Starkweather snapped the family dog's neck, killing it instantly.

Several hours later, C. Lauer Ward returned home. Upon walking in the back door, Starkweather was waiting for him with his shotgun.

Less than three feet into his home, Ward was shot in the head and killed. Caril and Charles then took all of the valuables in the house that they could find. This included jewelry, silver, gold, and art. They filled Lauer Ward's car up and sped off less than thirty minutes after killing him. The couple then drove straight across the state line out of Nebraska.

With all of the gruesome murder scenes being discovered in this short time period, Nebraska police departments, specifically Lancaster County, were scrambling for answers. Upon the Wards' murder discovery, a community lock down was issued. Each home was searched for possible leads and information. Their big break, however, was soon to come.

Having fled to Wyoming, the couple knew that they needed a new car. Ward's car drew too much attention and was wanted by law enforcement. The last murder of the killing spree was soon to take place. Traveling salesmen Merle Collison was asleep in his Buick on the side of the road. The couple drove by and realized their opportunity. Upon awakening Collison, Starkweather delivered a single shotgun blast to Collison's head. They had secured their new vehicle.

Popular culture focuses on this murder precisely for the actions of Caril Fugate. Caril reportedly performed a *coup-de-grace*. As Starkweather had an issue with his shotgun, Fugate supposedly delivered the fatal wound. While Fugate denies this, many believe this to be true. Charles Starkweather described her as "the most trigger happy person" he knew.

To Starkweather's luck, the salesmen's car that he had stolen had a unique push-pedal emergency brake system. He was completely unfamiliar with how to operate it. The car stalled repeatedly as the couple was making their getaway. A passing motorist stopped to offer assistance to the couple. He was immediately threatened with his life by Starkweather and his shotgun. A brief struggle ensued.

During the struggle, a deputy sheriff passed by the scene. As the sheriff exited his vehicle, Caril Fugate ran to the sheriff exclaiming, "It's Starkweather! He's going to kill me!" Starkweather jumped in the car and sped away. With officers in close pursuit, speeds in the chase exceeded 100 miles per hour. With gun blasts raining down on Starkweather's car, a stray bullet shattered the glass next to him causing lacerations. It was at this time that Charles Starkweather gave himself up.

"He thought he was bleeding to death. That's why he stopped. That's the kind of yellow son of a bitch he is," said Sheriff Earl Heflin.

Starkweather and Fugate were extradited back to Nebraska in late January 1958. Initially, he claimed that Fugate had no participation in the murders. After much questioning, his story changed numerous times. He would eventually agree that she was a willing participant.

Fugate claimed that she was held against her will. She claimed that her families lives were being threatened, and she had no idea that they were already dead. The judge firmly believed that she was an active participant. He felt that she had ample opportunity to escape. Caril Fugate was charged with murder and received a life sentence on November 21, 1958. She served 17 ½ years and was paroled. Caril moved to Michigan and changed her name. She married in 2007 and, despite a serious automobile accident that killed her husband and left her seriously injured, is still alive today. She has done only one major radio interview about the killing spree. She has stayed mute on the subject in her years after prison.

Charles Starkweather was found guilty of murder and given the death penalty. He was executed by way of the electric chair at 12:04 a.m. on June 25, 1959 at Nebraska State Penitentiary.

For just under two months, the crimes committed by Charles Starkweather and Caril Fugate can only be described as disturbing. Such senseless killing at the hands of a strange couple in the early years of their life. Many describe Starkweather as a stray dog. He is imaged this way as the animal that gets a taste of blood that can't seem to let it go. For Charles Starkweather and Caril Fugate, they got a taste of blood and strived to kill all that they could. If not for that sheriff driving by their struggle on the highway, the true numbers of this spree could have been exponentially higher. To anyone familiar with the case, Charles Starkweather got exactly what he deserved.

The Wolf Family Massacre

Carina David

The Wolf family massacre

The tale of the murders of Jacob Wolf, his wife and five children, and their hired help who was also a relative by marriage to the family is chilling, to say the least. The only survivor of this horrible crime was little baby Emma who was eight months old at the time of the murder.

There are many different theories out there today about what actually happened. Many people believe different things due to the complex case that it was. Henry Layer, a resident on a neighboring farm of the Wold family and was accused of the murder and sentenced to prison. Things got a bit complicated when he went on to sign 3 affidavits, the first where he admitted his guilt, and the last two when he was pleading his innocence. This caused a lot of tension at that time, and even now, and caused a lot of questions to come up.

It all started just a little while after the murder, two days to be exact. John Kraft and his wife drove into the yard of the Wolf farm. They hooted, and everything was deathly quiet, except they could hear the faint cry of a baby inside the Wolf family home. They hooted once again, and the baby gave a strong cry.

Nobody came out so Mr. Kraft and his wife went inside to investigate. As they walked into the kitchen, they saw no bodies but traces of blood that led to the cellar trap door. When they looked in, that is when they saw the bodies of Mrs. Wolf, three of her daughters and the body of Jakob Hofer, the hired help.

They later came upon the bodies of Mr. Wolf and his two oldest daughters which were covered in hay in the shed. John Kraft tried to phone someone for help but then he noticed the lines had been cut. They then took baby Emma who was worn out from hunger, crying and cold, back to their home to take care of her there. Reports say that she was very weak at that time. They phoned the police and that's when the investigation began. It was just two weeks after the crime when police took Henry Layer into custody and accused him of the murder of the Wolf family, eight victims in total.

In his first signed affidavit, his confession, he said that he left his home and went to see Mr. Wolf about an issue they had been having with Mr. Wolf's dogs. Apparently, the dog had bitten one of his cows and he wanted Mr. Wolf to come look at the cow to assess the damage done. He said that he walked into the house, into the kitchen where Mr. Wolf, his wife, his five children and their hired hand, Jakob Hofer were sitting.

Apparently, Mr. Wolf had told Layer to go away and that when Layer had refused to leave and tried to reason with him, that Mr. Wolf went to get his double-barrelled shotgun out of the front room. According to Layer, there was a struggle and then two shots were fired in a quick succession of one another. If this was the case, these were the two shots that killed Mrs. Wolf and the hired hand, Jakob Hofer. Mrs. Beata Wolf was thirty-five years of age. She was shot in the back at close range. Jacob was shot through the back of his neck, and the bullet severed his jugular vein.

Layer then managed to get the gun away from Mr. Wolf and went to the front room and then took more shotgun shells from where he saw Wolf take the first two shotgun shells from, and reloaded the gun and started shooting the rest of the family. He said he cannot remember who he shot first but he thinks that he started by shooting Mr. Wolf. He says that Mr. Wolf had started running towards the cowshed when he shot him the first time. There were two shots fired again. One at a long distance which went in his back, and the other so close that it ripped three of his ribs away from his spine.

Layer then claims that he then went into the cowshed and found two of Wolf's daughters, Maria and Edna, who were aged 9 and 7, hiding in the corner and that he shot them where they stood. Maria was shot in the back of the head behind her left ear. Edna was also shot in the back of her head at close range.

Apparently, Layer saw the little girls running from the house to the cow shed which is why he went there to kill them. Investigators confirm this as the window in their parents' room which is where they probably were folding clothes, was open wide enough for them to get through. There was also footprint evidence under the window.

Little Liddia who was about five years old at the time, was shot at the back of her left ear and had a second blow to her head with a hatchet. And the youngest victim, little Martha who was three years old was the only one who did not sustain wounds from a shotgun, instead, she died from a blow with the broad side of the hatchet blade to her head.

He went on to cover the bodies of the girls with hay and then placed Wolf on top of the girls and covered him with his coat and with more Hay. He then opened the trap door that lead from the kitchen to the basement and then he threw the rest of the bodies into the basement and then put down the trap door.

When asked why he did not kill baby Emma, he said it was because she was sleeping at the time of the incident and he did not go into that room. He pulled out the telephone wires and he left the house and closed the doors.

He said he picked up all the empty shells and carried them with him. He broke the gun and threw the broken gun and the shells into the slough. He said that he then went to his house which was approximately two miles away. He said he believed he got home about three hours after he had first gone to the Wolfs' farm.

He then added, at the end, as if it was an afterthought that when he finished shooting in the cowshed, he threw three or four empty shells into the hayloft through an open door. This was signed May 13, 1920, not even three weeks after the massacre.

The funeral

The funeral for the murdered family was held in Turtle Lake. There were over 2 500 people in attendance, even though turtle lake only had a total population of 395. People who had heard about the story came from far and wide. This type of crime was unheard of at that time, and up until this day, it remains one of the most horrendous mysteries and horrible murders of time.

At that time there was nobody in custody for the murder of the Wolf family and Jakob Hofer yet, but many had suspicions as to who the culprit might be. There are some reports that accused Henry of being the murder at the time. They say that Henry Layer opened the caskets and gazed at the faces of the dead family members. But, this was actually the norm back then. Everyone was expecting an open-casket funeral.

There were at least two people who helped prepare the bodies for the funeral as they knew that people would see them, so they wanted to make them look as decent and as respectable as possible. The bodies were so badly mutilated that it even caused one of the women who were helping to clean up the bodies faint. Everyone looked at the mutilated faces of the dead family, including Layer. The women held back shrieks and the men held back their tears. This was not a reason to suspect him at the time, although, after being accused of the murder, people did find it very scary that if he did kill them, he managed to look at all of their bodies after the time. This would have had to be a very sick person.

A separate service was held for Jakob Hofer, who was murdered along with the family. It was held at the farm home of his parents, Bernhardt and Caroline Hofer. He was buried with Jacob and Beata Wolf, as well as their five children at the Turtle Lake Cemetery.

Another theory.

Because of all the questions that came up and the fact that so many people were killed without anyone hearing anything lead to many people making up their own theories. Rumor at the time was that Mr. Wolf was having sexual relations with one of Layer's daughters. There was never ever evidence about this matter but that would have been the perfect motive.

Layer said that he entered the house to talk to Wolf which was also strange because it is well documented that Wolf had two very good sheepdogs which would have alerted him that there was someone at the farm gate. He would have then gone outside to see who it was. This was the custom in that day. No man would just walk into the home of another.

Reports from neighbors also show that the incident of the dogs biting Layer's cattle was not new and it had been ongoing for six months. Neighbors said that Layer and Wolf were not on talking terms. Wolf would not have let Layer into his house, into the kitchen where his wife and children were sitting if these were indeed the circumstances.

Layer says that he threw everybody into the cellar but as shown from pictures of the scene there was one puddle of blood in the kitchen. Also, the body of Jakob Hofer, the hired helper, was the only one that was on the floor right in front of the ladder, so he was the only one that would have been thrown down.

One of the theories is that the murders were committed during breakfast and not at noon. Also that Mrs. Wolf and her three daughters were not killed in the kitchen, but instead in the cellar where they might have been hiding, or made to go by the attackers.

Investigators found the body of Mrs. Wolf behind the ladder and contrary to the statement by Layer; the investigators had originally believed that Mrs. Wolf was indeed shot in the basement which would have made more sense because of where her body was found.

They then theorize that Hofer was probably coming into the kitchen in the morning, and was shot from behind. They then think that the oldest daughters had tried to run away after hearing the events in the kitchen, which is why they fled from the house and into the cow shed and they hid behind the haystack, which is where they were shot.

What was also suspicious was the fact that in his first statement he said that he threw the broken gun and all the shells in the slough, but afterwards he said that he had thrown more shells through an open door. They all landed in a chicken nest, neatly against each other.

The fact that he had said that in an afterthought was suspicious to some. Also the fact that he was the one that found them and reported them made people wonder that if he was the murderer, would he have not hid them instead of reporting it to the investigators. The fact that the shotgun shells were lying there led people to believe that there were two people involved in the massacre and that someone was waiting there for Bertha and Jacob to come from the fields on hearing the gunshots, and then killing them.

What was also questionable about his first statement was the fact that he said the first two shots that went off by accident were the ones to kill Mrs. Wolf and Jacob, although it is highly unlikely to have two accident shots go off and shoot two people. One was shot in the neck and the other behind the ear. There is no saying what distance they stood at and where they were positioned. It is plausible but unlikely.

According to Layer, the shotgun belonged to Mr. Wolf. The shotgun was found by one of the numerous neighbors that had gone to the farm the day after the murder had been reported. Nobody could verify that the shotgun did indeed belong to Wolf. His friends and relatives also did not recognize the gun.

The oldest daughter and Hofer had gloves on when they were killed, which were still on their hands when their bodies were found. This might show that they were working in the field before they were murdered.

Circumstances of the first confession.

On August 10th, Layer signed another affidavit in which he described the interrogation. He said that a few days after the funeral, four men came to his house and told him to go with them to talk about the killing.

While on their way to Washburn, they stopped and captured another man who Layer thought was an escaped convict from the prison. They put both of them in prison. The convict told Layer that he had a way to escape but Layer refused to go along with any of his plans. They saw each other often and the convict would always ask Layer why he was in prison. His reply was always the same – for no reason.

On May 12th, he went to the Sheriff's office and was questioned. This was no normal interview. Layer claims that he was continuously shown pictures of the murder scene. They carried on the interview until the early hours of the morning.

Layer claims that he was threatened. He was told that there was a mob outside waiting for him as they wanted to take the course of justice upon themselves. Apparently, he was told that the only way that he would ever survive was to confess to the crime and go to jail.

He said that they swore at him and took his chair away and made him stand to the point that he got dizzy. He kept saying he was innocent even through all of this. After that, one of the men in the room hit hum on the side of his head, took him by the hair and pulled him around the room.

Layer claims that this man then sat across the table from him and told him exactly how the murder happened, what he was to say, and then he got up, shook a club in his face and then threatened him by saying that if he did not say that, he would beat him to death.

Layer then gave up. He was crying and then said that he would do as they wished. They then called someone in to write down the confession.

More questions

An affidavit signed by a prison barber at the time confirmed the statements in the second affidavit of Layer.

When Henry Layer arrived at the State Penitentiary in Bismarck, North Dakota, that Myrle Cook had just started acting as a barber there. He said that he shaved Henry Layer and gave him a haircut. He said that when he started working on him, he saw that Layer was badly beaten up and that both sides of his face and the top of his head were swollen and it was obvious that he had been beaten by someone.

He asked Layer what had happened. In reply, Layer told him that he was beaten by the man who had charge of him before he was brought to the institution. He apparently broke down and cried very much and kept on saying that he was innocent.

Dr. C. E. Stackhouse said under oath that he had examined Layer and found him to be in a "normal physical condition". He said that there were two areas of ecchymosis on his face, one over each cheek bone and about the size of a silver dollar but that there was no swelling.

Both these affidavits from these persons show that there must have been some sort of incident. But one describes it as not such a big deal, whereas the other said that Layer had been badly beaten and that there was swelling. Will we ever know the truth?

An affidavit signed by Layer's brother-in-law, William Brokofsky was also in support of Layer's petition for a change of plea. William and Henry's wife, Lydia, went to the State Penitentiary of Bismarck, North Dakota to go see Henry on the first Sunday after he was committed. They asked to see and talk to him but they were refused. They were told that Henry was not in a condition to be seen.

A short while after, they went again to see him. This time they got to see and talk to Henry. This was the first time that William had a chance to talk to him since his confinement and Henry kept on telling him he was innocent. He had also told him under which circumstances he had to admit to the crime.

Lydia Layer also signed an affidavit dated December 20, 1920, which said that she and Henry were married and they were well acquainted with the Wold family. The said that she was at home all day on the 22nd of April, and did the usual work which was hers to do.

She said that she knew of her husband's whereabouts and that Henry was working in the fields that day and that he never left the farm during any part of the day. She said that at noon, at the usual hour, Henry came home and ate and then returned to work which was the usual.

Physical evidence – or the lack thereof

There was no physical evidence that could connect Layer to the murders. The case was wrapped up quickly because people were terrified and others wanted the case to be closed quickly.

More about the accused

Henry Layer, born Heinrich C. Layer was born on the 12 of November 1884 is Eigenfeld, South Russia. HE moved to the country in 1886. Lydia was his second wife. His first wife was Mathilda Miller. They had two children who went by the names of Elizabeth Katherina and Edward. The couple was divorced in March 1911 and the children stayed with their mother.

He went on to marry Lydia Brokofsky Hinzman in January 1912. He was sentenced to life in prison on May 13th, 1920. He and his wife were divorced on December 21, 1922. It is believed that they were divorced so that Layer could free his wife from any legal obligations towards him and that she could move on. Layer then died in hospital on March 21, 1925, after having a blood clot go through his heart after receiving an appendectomy. His wife then remarried only after his death, in November 1925.

Authorities said that Layer was a model prisoner and that he had acted as the head man in the laundry. The obituary stated that he was buried in a local cemetery but up until this day, it is not known exactly where he was buried.

Who was Jakob Hofer?

Jakob was the son of Bernhardt Hofer, who is a brother to Emanuel Whober, who married the sister of Beata Wolf, Christina Bossert. He was only thirteen years old at the time of the incident. He is often referred to as the hired help because Mr. Jakob Wolf had hired him to help him with the spring plantation after a boy who was supposed to help him had to decline. He was in fact family.

What happened to little baby Emma?

The incident happened when baby Emma was just eight months old. She was found just in time because she was so weak already from all the crying, the cold, and going without food or anything to drink. Even though her life was spared, one can just think what kind of an impact that would have had on the rest of her life.

Emma was in attendance at the funeral of her family at that very young age. She lived with her mother's sister and her husband but they passed away in the 1930's. After that, she was put into the guardianship of a couple who lived near her hometown, Turtle Lake. She later went on to study teaching.

Emma carried on to live her entire life in the Turtle Lake area. She was married in 1940 to a gentleman named Clarence Hanson. They had three children. Emma lived a happy life and she died on the 16th of October, 2003 at the advanced age of 84.

More tragedy struck

After her husband had gone to prison and they divorced, 5 of the six Layer children went to an orphanage in Minnesota, and only the youngest that was a year old at that stage had stayed with his mother. One of their children, Berthold Layer was killed at age 6. While at the orphanage the children were playing at one of the farm gates.

According to the Fairmont Sentinel, little Berthold had been told to stay away from the wagon that was coming in with sugar beets on the back. All of a sudden the driver, F.C Fuller, felt the back of the wagon lift up.

Berthold must have fallen underneath it and it drove over him. His skull had cracked at its' base and his death was said to be instant. His siblings, two brothers, and one sister, who had seen what happened. The youngest who was 4 at the time, Edwin, could not understand it and just cried while he tried to console his siblings, Blanche and his brothers Alvin and Emil.

A twist to the tale

In mid-November 1920, new evidence was found on the Wolf farm. John Hofer and his wife and four children were now renting the land. While playing outside, two of the young children made a thrilling discovery. In some bushes not too far from the house, wrapped in an oil tablecloth, were two homemade cloth masks, a woman's worn dusting cap, and a shotgun shell.

The one mask was large and had holes for the eyes and mouth. Another, smaller mask only had holes for the eyes. The empty shotgun shell was identical to the one found at the scene of the crime. One of the masks and the dusting cap had blood on them.

It is believed that this evidence was planted because hundreds of neighbors came to comb over the farm to look for evidence and investigators are sure they would have found it. But it was planted, or just missed; it is believed that these objects were related to the murder. It is believed that these objects could belong to a man and a woman. Are they the murderers? Or were they involved in the murders?

Conclusion

There are certainly some unanswered questions about this case. Many people were hurt by these events. The Wolf family, the Layer family, the Hofer family, and all the people that knew and loved them. It had quite an impact on all the children at that time, as we can only imagine. The murder tore families apart and it still causes confusion to this day. Will we ever know the answers to these questions? Will justice ever be served? Maybe it already has been, and perhaps, it never will be.

THE JUST DO IT KILLER

SARAH THOMPSON

McCamey, Texas. A town of less than two thousand people, out in the scorching Texas desert, where downtown is a stretch of black road with marginally more buildings on either side. McCamey is the type of town that lies, more or less, entirely forgotten by the rest of the United States, down in the deep heat of Texas. It was in McCamey, in 1940, that Gary Mark Gilmore was born. Gilmore would have, perhaps, gone one to live and die a completely unnoticed life if circumstances had been different. As it stands, Gary Mark Gilmore would gain fame through his life for being the first person sentenced to death in the United States in nearly ten years for the crimes that he committed.

On December 4th, in 1940, Frank and Bessie Gilmore became the parents of their second son, Gary Mark Gilmore. Frank and Bessie were married on a whim, and Frank was said to have other wives and families that he otherwise ignored. Bessie was a Mormon from Provo, Utah, but she had been outcast by her community. Bessie and Frank met and married in California, but the both of them eventually moved to McCamey, Texas, where Gary Mark had been born. Gilmore would have three brothers: Frank Jr., Gaylen and Mikal Gilmore. It was in McCamey that Frank and Bessie were living with their first son Frank Jr., and existing under the false name of "Coffman" in order to escape detection from law enforcement. When he was born, Gary Mark Gilmore had been given the name Faye Robert Coffman - Faye, named after Frank Gilmore Sr.'s mother, Fay.

However, the name Faye Robert didn't stick. His mother, Bessie, decided to change it to Gary Mark Gilmore after they left Texas. Moving wasn't uncommon for the Gilmore family. Gary spent most of his childhood moving from city to city throughout most of the Western United States, along with this three brothers and his parents.

Frank Gilmore supported the family during this time with the sale of fraudulent magazine subscriptions. Gary's relationship with his father was rocky, as was the rest of the family's relationship with Frank Gilmore, Sr. He was described as a man with a quick temper, and who was easily angered. He was also a strict father, and one to dole out corporal punishment when and if he saw fit. Frank often did not need a reason to beat his sons, and would routinely whip them with a razor strop, belt or whip.

Frank Gilmore, Sr. did not only take out his anger and violence on his sons. Though this was less frequent, he would also take to beating Bessie. The relationship between Frank and Bessie was also volatile. Gary grew up in a household in which his parents would often take to screaming at one another, and verbally abusing one another with insults and digs at each other's religions. Bessie would even threatened to kill Frank Sr. some nights. The two parental figures of the household were constantly at one another's throats, and it was the source of a lot of distress and frustration and turmoil within the Gilmore family.

Exposure to violence between his mother and father and the crimes of his father did nothing for Gary's disposition. While his other brothers seemed to escape the thrall of their household unscathed, Gary wasn't so lucky. There's no telling what a calmer household would have done for Gary, and if his rocky home life was the root cause for the crimes he would commit and the path he would soon begin to take in life.

Despite the Gilmore family's nomadic lifestyle for the greater part of Gary's children, they finally settled down in Portland, Oregon in the year 1952. Gary was twelve at the time, and like most twelve year olds, he was starting to stretch his legs and discover some semblance of independence and self-identity. During his adolescence, Gary was incredibly intelligent. He tested an IQ score of 133, and throughout his schooling career he tested and scored well on both aptitude and achievement tests. Gary even showed an incredible ability for artistic talent. He was on the entirely right track to being a successful student and graduating from school.

Unfortunately, Gary did not continue down this path. He was in the ninth grade when he decided to drop out of high school. It was then that Gary became caught up in petty crimes, and took to anti-social behaviors. After he dropped out of high school, Gary ran away from home with a friend. They traveled from Oregon all the way down to Texas. There they stayed for several months before finally returning back to Portland. It was at 14 that he finally managed to succumb to his first arrest. He had started a car theft ring with some friends. Rather than put him in jail, law enforcement released him back to his father and all Gary received from police was a slap on the wrist and a warning to keep in line.

Gary didn't take either the warning or the gift seriously. It wasn't any more than two weeks later when Gary found himself back in court on yet another charge for car theft. At this point, the court sent Gary to the MacLaren Reform School for Boys. The MacLaren Reform School was a correctional facility located in Woodburn, Oregon. The boys residing in MacLaren were anywhere from age 13 to 25, and had committed and range of crimes. In retrospect, due to Gary's immense intelligence and his own willful nature, it might have been the fact that he was sent to MacLaren that had redoubled his affinity for crime, or at least his unwillingness to stop.

Gary was released the next year from MacLaren, but he didn't stay out for long. For the next several years, Gary would be in and out of prison for various crimes. In 1960, at 20 years old, Gary was convicted of another car theft. This time, he was sentenced to time in the Oregon State Correctional Institute. He served a minimal amount of time there, and was even released later in the year. It was around this time in 1961, that Gary's father, Frank Gilmore Sr., was diagnosed with lung cancer. It was terminal. Gary's tumultuous relationship with his father was coming to an end.

In 1962, Gary was once more arrested. This time, the crime was much more severe than stealing a car. He was charged with armed robbery and assault, and was sentenced to Oregon State Penitentiary. It was during this stint in prison that Frank Gilmore Sr. passed away from lung cancer. Gary was in prison at the time and was unable to say goodbye, or even receive the news directly from his family. One of the guards that the Oregon State Penitentiary gave Gary the news about his father's passing.

Gary's relationship with his father had never been good. He grew up in a household where his father and mother were always at odds, with him and his brother's caught in the middle. Frank Gilmore, Sr. was brutal, violent and strict on his sons. He went beyond disciplining them when he raised his belt or whip against Gary and his brothers. Mikal had even once described their father as a "cruel and unreasonable man". And yet, despite all of that - despite the years spent moving around at the whim of his con man father, and despite the years spent at the end of a leather strop and watching his father beat his mother, Gary Gilmore was distraught over the old man's death. When he was given the news of Frank Sr.'s passing, Gary tried to end his life by slitting his wrists.

The suicide attempt was unsuccessful, and Gary Gilmore remained alive. He was eventually released back into suicide. For two years, Gary either stayed out of trouble or managed not to get caught. And yet, in 1964, Gary was once more returned to prison - on the charges of armed robbery and assault, once more. This time, Gary was sentenced to fifteen years in prison for his habitual offenses. A prison psychiatrist finally diagnosed Gary with antisocial personality disorder as well as something called intermittent psychotic decompensation. Psychotic decompensation is a term that describes the rapid deterioration of someone's mental health that they had been, up until then, been otherwise maintaining. This, along with Gary's personality disorder characterized by his disregard and often violation of other people's rights and autonomy, make him a perfect package for crime.

By the time he was 30, Gary Gilmore had spent the greater part of his adult life in and out of prison. The intelligence that had heard him such high marks and a promising future when he was a boy didn't disappear over the years. In fact, Gary used much of his time in prison to write poetry and make artwork. It was these talents that initially won Gary conditional release to a halfway house in Eugene, Oregon. In 1972, he was granted permission to live weekdays at the halfway house under the condition that he stay out of trouble and take art classes at the local community college. However, in line with Gary's usual behavior, he ended up never registering for classes at the community college. Within a month of his initial conditional release, Gary Gilmore couldn't resist the siren call of crime, and was once more arrested and convicted on the charge of armed robbery.

Gary Gilmore's behavior in prison turned from quiet poetry crafting to violence, and he was eventually transferred to a maximum-security federal prison in Marion, Illinois. He was transferred there in 1975. Now 35, it was looking like Gary Gilmore would be spending many more years of is still short life in prison. While he was serving his time in Marion, Gary began writing letters with his cousin, Brenda Nicol. Perhaps it was through Gary's particular intelligence that he manipulated her into believing he deserved a second change, or maybe it was Brenda's own idea. All the same, in 1976, Gary was once more given conditional release into the care of his cousin, Brand. He would live with her in Provo, Utah, under the condition that he stay out of trouble. Brenda would help him look for work and aid in his reform, offering Gary a support system that he had not had previously.

Gary began working at a shoe repair store owned by his uncle, Vern Damico. He also worked, briefly, for an insulation company. This rehabilitation seemed to be on the up and up, and Gary's life was being steered clear of all his previous habits. Unfortunately, Gary wasn't able to keep away from his old ways for long. Soon after his foray into a new life, Gary was back into his old habits of drinking, stealing and fighting. He got into a relationship with a 19 year old woman by the name of Nicole Baker. Nicole was both a window and a divorcee and she had two young children at the time that she and Gary got together. Their relationship was casual at first, but it didn't take long for things between Gary and Nicole to become both intense and strained. Perhaps it was from his own parent's relationship that Gary had learned how to interact with others in a romantic sense - that is, he didn't learn very well at all.

Gary soon began imitate his father. He became controlling with Nicole, and threatening. Their relationship was strained both from Gary's violent behavior, as well as pressure from Nicole's family for her to leave him. Gary was having trouble adjusting to life outside of prison, after spending nearly half of his life, and almost all of his adult life, behind bars. His relationship with Nicole was just a precursor to Gary's inevitable inability to reform himself and stay the straight and narrow path.

It all came to a head on July 19th, 1976. Gary Gilmore stopped at a gas station in Orem, Utah. He had been travelling at the time with April, Nicole Baker's younger sister. During this time, Gary and Nicole were still off-again on-again, in an unstable and volatile relationship. It was around 10:30 in the evening that Gary stopped and told April that he needed to make a phone call. He left April in the car and entered the gas station. It was there that he robbed the gas station attendant, Max Jensen, at gunpoint, continuing his affinity for armed robbery. This time, however, Gary took it another step. After Gary had instructed Jensen to give him the money box, he forced him into the bathroom and had him lay down on the floor. Max Jensen obeyed all of Gary's demands, but his obedience was for naught. According to Gary's confession of the crime, he held his gun against Jensen's head and said,

"This one is for me," before firing the gun once. He then stated, "For Nicole", before firing the gun a second time, shooting Jensen twice and then leaving him, dead and bleeding, on the bathroom floor of the gas station.

Leaving Orem behind, Gary traveled back to Provo with April and spent the night in a motel nearby where he left his truck in a service garage to be repaired. The evening after his armed robbery and murder in Orem, Gary robbed a hotel manager by the name of Ben Bushnell, who lived on the property with his family. Much like the victim before him, Ben Bushnell complied with every one of Gary's demands. An eyewitness, motel guest Peter Arroyo, would later describe Gary ordering Bushnell to lie on the floor. Much like Jensen, Bushnell was shot and killed. When he tried to dispose of his weapon that he used in both robberies and murders, Gary managed to accidentally shoot himself in his right hand. Had he not, he might have managed to get away with both killings and continue on to commit more escalated violence. As it were, his bleeding hand alerted the garage mechanic, Michael Simpson, who had seen Gary trying to hide the gun in the nearby bushes.

Michael Simpson wrote down Gary's license plate number after hearing about a shooting at a nearby motel on a police scanner. He called the police and alerted them of the goings on, of Gary's wounded hand and of his disposing of the gun in the bushes by the mechanic garage. Meanwhile, Gary had called his cousin for support, but she was unsympathetic to his plight. She called the police as well, and Gary was taken into custody after law enforcement found him at the edge of town not long after the incident.

Gary Mark Gilmore isn't the most prolific killer in history, or even of his time. He probably wouldn't even be classified as a serial killer, or even a spree killer. It's Gary's particular circumstances that make him so famous, however. It was the same year that Gary Mark Gilmore was arrested for two counts of murder that the U.S Supreme Court upheld a series of new death penalty statutes in the court decision of Gregg v. Georgia. Before that, death penalty statutes had been deemed "cruel and unusual punishment", and therefore deemed unconstitutional. It wasn't until the 1976 Supreme Court decision that the death penalty was reinstated. Perhaps, if this ruling had not occurred, Gary Mark Gilmore would have rotted away in life in prison as many others had before him during the time where the death penalty was not in effect. Gary Mark Gilmore was charged with both the murders of Jensen and Bushnell, though only Bushnell's murder actually went to trial, due to a lack of evidence and eyewitnesses to Jensen's murder—even though Gary admitted to both.

He was held in custody until October 5th, 1976. It was on that day that Gary Mark Gilmore's trail began in Provo. It lasted only two days. Unhappy with his lawyers' lack of cross-examination and lack of their own witnesses for his defense, Gary persuaded the judge to let him take the stand in his own defense. He claimed dissociation and lack of control, and tried to make a case of insanity. His own attorney's called four separate psychiatrists to shoot down this attempt of claiming insanity, showing that Gary had full control and awareness of what he was doing during the crimes. Not even his antisocial personality disorder was enough for him to actually meet the legal definition of insanity. Despite his intelligence and his skilled manipulation tactics, Gary was not able to present a defense for himself. It seemed that he knew when he was beat.

On October 7, 1976, after two days of trial, the jury returned a guilty verdict. They also agreed on the death penalty, due to circumstances surrounding Gary's crimes. This would be the first execution in the United States in ten years, and the first execution that would happen after the Supreme Court decision to allow the death penalty once more.

Gary's mother, Bessie, attempted to sue to for a stay of execution, despite the fact that Gary himself chose not to pursue habeas corpus.

In a unanimous decision, the U.S Supreme Court refused to even hear Bessie's claim, and her son was slated to be executed. A death penalty sentence in modern times includes lethal injection, as it has been proven to be the most humane way of sentencing a criminal to death, unlike the methods of the past such as hanging or the electric chair. During Utah in 1976, however, the only methods available for executions were hanging, or a firing squad. Gary Mark Gilmore had already accepted his fate as the first man to be executed in the United States in almost ten years. To Gary, a hanging had room for error. He told the court, "I prefer to be shot," and chose the firing squad. Thus, his execution was set for 8 am on November 15th.

Despite having accepted his fate, Gary ended up actually receiving a few stays of execution, though he did not seek them out and explicitly did not want them. It was at the hands of the American Civil Liberties Union (ACLU) and his attorneys that drew out his already chosen execution. When his lawyers tried to call of an appeal on his case, Gary opted instead to fire them. He was ready to face his death, and he saw no reason to draw it out any longer. It was this refusal of appeal that drew the ACLU's attention. The ACLU made efforts, hand in hand with the National Association for the Advancement of Colored People to turn over Gary's execution. However, it wasn't entirely for Gary's benefit. They were using Gary's case to benefit the prisoners who were standing on death row throughout the United States, all of whom were now in danger of facing execution now that the Supreme Court had reinstated the death penalty.

Gary's execution got tied up in legalities. He was ready for it to all be over. In November 1976, while Gary was taking part in a Board of Pardons hearing, Gary said this of all the legal attempts to spare his life: "It's been sanctioned by the courts that I die and I accept that." The dragged out legal battle between the courts and the ACLU put off Gary's execution for months, and in the interim Gary attempted suicide twice. His first attempted occurred on November 16th when his first stay of execution was announced. Nicole Barrett visited Gary in prison, despite her having broken off their relationship. They kissed and held one another during Nicole's visit, and the reason for it became clear. Nicole had snuck in sleeping pills. After she had left, Gary swallowed the overdose of pills—while at the same time, miles away in her own home, Nicole Barrett had done the same, the both of them attempting suicide. Gary had not taken enough sleeping pills for the dosage to be fatal. Nicole took a larger dosage of sleeping pills, which resulted in her slipping into a coma for several days. Gary was not finished with attempting to end his life. With or without Nicole, Gary attempted suicide again one month later to the exact day in December. When that didn't work, he took up a hunger strike.

Finally, Gary was given a date for execution: January 17th, 1977. On the night before his execution, Gary requested that he be allowed to have an all-night gathering that consisted of his friends and family. He was granted the request, and spent his last evening surrounded by the people in his life that could be considered his loved ones. Gary's last meal consisted of potatoes and steak to eat, and milk and coffee to drink. For whatever reason, Gary didn't touch his steak and potatoes. The last thing that he had was the milk and the coffee. The next morning, on January 17th, Gary's last stay of execution was overturned at 7:30 AM, and Gary was finally allowed to go through with his execution as he had wanted so many months previously.

At 8:07 AM, Gary was taken behind the prison to an abandoned cannery. He was placed and secured into a chair with a wall of sandbags behind him for the purpose of absorbing the bullets. In tradition of firing squad, five local police were placed behind a cloth with only a small hole for them to put through the barrel of their rifles, aimed directly at his body from 20 feet away. In Utah tradition, the firing squad consists of four men with live rounds and one man with a blank round. This is done, ostensibly, so that the men comprised of the firing squad will never know which one of them fired the killing shot.

When he was asked for any last words, all Gary Mark Gilmore had to say was this: "Let's do it!" A black hood was placed on his head, and the five gunmen were allowed to fire a single bullet into the body of the first man to undergo execution in the United States in almost ten years. Gary's youngest brother, Mikal Gilmore, was allowed to inspect the clothes worn by his brother after his execution. Allegedly, there were five holes left in the clothes, not four. He noted this in his memoir, 'Shot in the Heart', and mused that Utah wanted to take no chances on leaving his brother alive. Mikal's memoir goes in depth into his relationship with Gary, as well as the strained relationship he had with his family, as well as the aftermath of his own brother's execution at the hands of the state of Utah.

Before his death, Gary had requested that his organs be donated to those in need of transplant. Because of his death by firing squad, it can be presumed that some of his internal organs were useless, now riddled with bullet holes - mainly, his heart, where a piece of black cloth had been pinned as a target for the firing squad. Strangely enough, though, two people were able to receive corneal transplants, courtesy of now famed murderer Gary Mark Gilmore. After his autopsy, Gary's body was cremated. In a grandiose decision by his family, Gary's ashes were then scattered from an airplane over Spanish Fork, Utah.

Gary Mark Gilmore is notorious, perhaps not for his crimes, but for when his crimes occurred. He would have otherwise rotted away in prison, unknown but for the people whose lives he had touched, no matter how horrid and terrible that touch may be. It was by virtue of the place and time that he had committed his crimes that gained Gary Mark Gilmore his fame of being the first man executed in the United States since the death penalty had been reinstated. It is more than just those who were involved in his case and legal battles that remember his name. Gary Mark Gilmore is now known for his own battle for execution. He is remembered in both the minds of those involved, as well as the legal histories of the United States.

The Texarkana Moonlight Murders

IRIS HULSE

Texarkana has always been an unusual place. On the east, you have Texarkana, Arkansas, a small town by any other measurement, yet home to the largest population in Miller County. To the west lies Texarkana, Texas, located in rural Bowie County and lucky enough to have its very own Wal-Mart. Together these twin cities make up what is simply referred to as "Texarkana."

Texarkana is a dusty town, built on a foundation of competing railroads and a Mexican border dispute in the 1800s. The town laid low for the next several years, sending off its sons to fight World War I and then II, and welcoming them back home for better or for worse. But no one in Texarkana was prepared for the national attention that came in the spring of 1946. On February 22nd, 1946, a masked serial killer, dubbed the "Phantom Killer" by the *Texarkana Gazette*'s Calvin Sutton, began terrorizing young couples on the town's secluded country roads.

Today, if you search the Internet for information on Texarkana and its morbid history, you will likely be redirected to pages on *The Town That Dreaded Sundown* and its Arkansan producer, Charles B. Pierce. In 1977, decades after the last murders, this film joined the ranks of *Halloween* and *The Texas Chainsaw Massacre* as one of Hollywood's classic horrors, featuring countless local residents as set extras. While the film's accuracy is something to be questioned, it remains a key piece of the town's identity. Visitors can even catch a screening every Halloween at Spring Lake Park, not far from where one of the infamous murders took place.

Texarkana may have embraced its celebrity status, but eighty years ago the town was paralyzed in fear. Within a single spring, five were dead and three were wounded. All in what had previously been a quiet, friendly community.

A Masked Attacker

Just before midnight, on February 22nd, 1946, Jimmy Hollis and Mary Jeanne Larey were finishing up their date in the backseat of

Hollis' father's car. Hollis, 24, and Larey, 19, had been dating for a while, but his parents expected the car (and the lovebirds) home by midnight. Throwing caution to the wind, they parked on a secluded dirt road, known as a lovers' lane, and proceeded to do what young couples will do.

The pair was soon startled by a flashlight, shining through the driver side window and blinding them to whoever stood outside. Hollis quickly composed himself and opened the door, thinking they were being interrupted by an ill-timed police patrol or a prank from some local kids, but they found themselves face-to-face with a masked man holding a gun.

Hollis continued to confront the intruder, telling him, "Fellow, you've got me mixed up with someone else. You got the wrong man." Hollis later said that the masked man muttered something like, "I don't want to kill you, so do what I say." Hollis attempted to calm the assailant, who forced the young man out of the vehicle and demanded Hollis remove his pants, gun pointed squarely at his face. Larey pleaded with Hollis to do as the man said, thinking he would not become violent if they did as he said. Instead the masked man overpowered Hollis, beating him over the head with the revolver. As Hollis lay limp on the cold ground, the attack continued until the sound of Hollis' skull cracking echoed throughout the clearing.

At this point Larey was hysterical with panic, thinking the loud crack of Hollis' broken skull was the sound of him being shot. She told the man they had no money or valuables, attempting to hand the man Hollis' wallet, but he only screamed, "Liar," at her and demanded her purse. Then the masked man told her to run toward the road. Larey ran as fast as she could, but the strange man pursued, continuing to scream, "Liar," at her as she ran.

The assailant eventually outpaced Larey, and forced her to the ground. Larey reported that the man did not rape her, but that assaulted her violent and used his gun to sexually molest her. Larey was afraid for her life, fighting against the weight of her attacker. She eventually managed to escape his grasp, rising up and telling him, "Go ahead and kill me." She then ran to a nearby house at 805 Blanton Street, where she managed to wake up the sleeping woners and pleaded for help. Shortly after, the Bowie County Sheriff, W.H. "Bill" Presley, arrived at what would be the first known Phantom Killer crime scene.

Hollis and Larey were lucky enough to survive this first attack, though they were left with plenty of physical and emotional scars to show for it. Hollis and Larey described their attacker as a tall man wearing a burlap sack with two slits cut for the eyes, though they could not agree on the man's race. Hollis believed the man was white, with tanned skin from working outdoors, while Larey insisted he was a black man because of his mannerisms and "curses." At this point, the attack was treated as a random attempted robbery, it was unknown the chaos that the Phantom Killer would bring in coming months.

The First Kill

In the early hours of March 24th, a truck driver spotted a young man asleep in an Oldsmobile parked on the side of the road. Concerned about the danger of passing traffic, the truck driver ran up to the window, hoping to wake the man and advise him of a better resting area. To the truck driver's horror, the young man was not asleep; he had been shot twice in the back of the head and sat dead in the driver's seat. In the Oldsmobile's backseat was a teenage girl wrapped in a bloody blanket, her body was completely lifeless. These young lovers were not as lucky as the Phantom Killer's first victims.

Richard Griffin, 29, was a retired Navy SeaBee on a double date with his girlfriend of six weeks, Polly Ann Moore, 17, when they pulled over on the highway to have some time alone. They had just finished up dinner with Griffin's sister and her boyfriend at a local café, and Griffin was in no rush to return his girlfriend to her parents' house. Unfortunately, they would never make it home.

Sometime that previous night, Griffin and Moore had pulled over onto the side of the road. It is believed they were approached similarly to the Phantom Killer's first victims, with a blinding flashlight and pointed gun. There was a heavy rainfall over Texarkana that night, so no one would have been out and about to see the killings take place.

Griffin was likely killed first, with two shots from a .32 Colt revolver to the back of his head. Moore, however, had been dragged from the vehicle and sexually assaulted on the cold, wet ground by their attacker. Blood and marks littered the dirt next to the vehicle. After this horror, Moore was also shot and killed by the Phantom Killer. The assailant pulled a blanket from the car's trunk and wrapped her in it before placing her body in the backseat of the Oldsmobile. Any fingerprints and footprints left behind by the killer that night was washed away by the storm.

Griffin's pockets were found empty and turned inside out, and Moore's purse remained at the scene but was emptied of any cash. With the only apparent motive being robbery, questions still remained as to why the crime was carried out so violently. The *Texarkana Gazette*, at the insistence of the Sheriff Bill Presley, made an announcement on March 27th asking residents to not spread rumors or anything else that they did not see with their own two eyes. Despite offering a cash reward, no solid tips ever made it to the police force.

Murder in the Park

Betty Jo Booker, 15, was a straight-A student who was adored by those around her. She worked with Jerry Atkins playing saxophone for a local band, The Rhythmaires, every Saturday night at the local VFW club. On April 14th, she and Atkins, as well as the rest of their band mates, were playing one of their normal shows. Every other weekend, Atkins gave Booker a ride home alternating with a band mate named Ernie Holcomb. This night was Holcomb's night to drive her home, but Booker told Holcomb not to bother because she had a ride set up with an old classmate who was visiting, Paul Martin. Atkins never knew of this change of plans, and until he received a call the next morning he assumed Booker had left with Holcombe, as usual.

Martin's 1946 Ford Coupe was found at 6:30 the next morning by the Weaver family, who were on their way through Texarkana to Prescott, Arkansas. The keys were found still in the car's ignition. Several miles away, in Spring Lake Park, their bodies would be found. Neither the car nor their bodies were anywhere near their destination that night.

Band and classmates claimed that the two were never close to being a couple, and that Booker felt obligated to go out with Martin because of their connection at school. However, no one knows what they were doing pulled over that night, or why they were in that area of town in the first place. No matter what the true story was that night, Booker and Martin would be the Phantom Killer's third and fourth victims.

Like the previous attack, both victims were shot and killed with a .32 Colt semi-automatic revolver. And like the female targets before her, Booker had been sexually assaulted before her murder. After news of the murder was released, hundreds of Texarkana residents flooded the park, hoping to catch a glimpse of the crime scene or help the investigation.

Martin's body was found almost a mile and a half from the abandoned car. He had been shot four times and the ground surrounding his body was covered in his blood.

Booker's body would not be found until five hours later, over three miles from where the car had been found. Booker was found by the Boyd family and Ted Schoeppey, who had joined the community search party to help find the two teenage victims. Booker had been shot twice, and was found with her hand in her coat pocket.

Both bodies showed signs of a struggle against their attacker, yet their fight was unsuccessful. There was no conclusive evidence as to why their bodies were so far from their car.

Booker's missing saxophone played in the running theory of robbery as a primary motive. The police had alerts al over the area, asking people to keep an eye out for a pawned or for sale saxophone matching the serial number of Booker's, and for several months it was considered one of the best leads the authorities had on finding the killer. Unfortunately for the police, on October 24th, six months after Booker's murder, P. V. Ward and J. F. McNief found the saxophone still in its leather case, just yards from where Booker's body had been found. Ward claimed to know what it was as soon as they stumbled upon it. By the time the case and instrument were turned over to the police, the case had already been labeled closed.

A Red Herring

Public panic over the Phantom Killer was at its all-time high when Virgil and Katie Starks were attacked in their modest farmhouse just ten miles out of town. However, questions would eventually emerge over whether this was truly the work of the Phantom Killer, or if someone else was responsible for the crime.

On the quiet night of May 3^{rd,} Virgil, 36, was reading the Texarkana Gazette when two gunshots burst through the front window of their ranch-style home. These bullets hit Virgil in the head, killing him instantly. Katie was lying in bed, already dressed in her nightgown, when she heard the sound of breaking glass. She headed for the living room, where her husband had been seated, only to find him slumped in his armchair, dead. She cried in fear as she reached for the phone, but the attacker shot through her lower jaw, spraying teeth fragments across the Starks kitchen.

In a state of panic and extreme pain, Katie managed to get back up to her feet. She attempted to grab her husband's gun, but was disoriented from being shot. Despite her injuries, she escaped from the house and ran for her sister's down the street. Finding the house empty, she continued to her neighbors' until she found refuge in the Prater house, where the police were finally called. When A. V. Prater answered the door, Katie simply said, "Virgil's dead," before collapsing on the ground. In the time it took for the police to arrive the killer had fled, taking no valuables or anything else of note with him. Initially, this attack was labeled as another of the Phantom Killer's. It followed the same time pattern as his previous attacks, used a gun as the primary weapon, and targeted a couple. One of the biggest pieces of evidence connecting this attack to the Phantom Killer was a set of unfamiliar tire tracks that matched those found at the other crime scenes. Because of these similarities, many citizens of Texarkana insist that this murder and attempted assault was the Phantom Killer's final blow to the small town's community.

In November 1948, the local authorities made a different conclusion. Another man was arrested and charged with the home invasion and attack on Virgil and Katie Starks. Law enforcement referenced several reasons as to this not being the work of the Phantom Killer, including the fact that the weapon used was a .22 rifle. This change in weapon, as well as the fact this was a home invasion earlier in the evening, pointed police to consider a different suspect entirely.

The town is still home to many skeptics who believe this attack was the Phantom Killer's doing. The crime scene at the Starks home was filled with physical DNA evidence, but at the time DNA testing was only beginning to emerge in the most developed areas of the nation. A little town like Texarkana was nowhere near equipped to handle a case like this, and the DNA evidence was discarded or improperly stored for later testing. While the official stance is that the Phantom Killer was not involved in this attack, the question still haunts many in the area.

A Town In Panic

As the attacks added up, tension in the town of Texarkana grew. After the first and second attack, police forces from both states increased patrols on the town's secluded back roads. A community that had once been friendly, where front doors were never locked and neighbors were always welcome, now grew eerily quiet after sundown.

Businesses saw a decline in customers, especially those catering to the night crowd. Residents were afraid to leave home, even during the daylight, for fear they may become the next target of the Phantom Killer. However, one industry in town became a hotspot for concerned citizens – the local hardware and ammo shops.

Residents bought up guns and ammo like crazy, hoping to be able to defend themselves from the attacks. Deadbolts and other home security devices became commonplace in all the towns households, and some homeowners were even seen setting up booby traps and other contraptions to catch the killer in his tracks.

Many of the town's local high school and college boys rounded up patrol groups. These men would go out at night with baseball bats and other makeshift weapons, hoping to catch the Phantom Killer on the prowl. None of them were ever successful.

Rumors continued to spread and impair the investigations. There was constant news about someone's son being arrested for the murders, or a suspect being charged, but these rumors rarely ever revealed themselves to be true. Police were forced to perform damage control on the stories spreading around town while also conducting their own investigation into the attacks.

Under the Spotlight

After the final attack, at the Starks farmhouse, authorities and media swarmed into Texarkana like never before. The quiet town was buzzing with news reporters from all across the nation, and reports of the murders were spreading to all areas of the country. Texarkana had never experienced the media's curious eye before.

The famous Texas Rangers stepped into the investigation, headed by the well-known Manuel "Lone Wolf" Gonzaullas. Gonzaullas was the first Ranger captain from Spanish descent, and was known for being a ruthless charmer in his day. He spent a great of his time providing interviews for national newspapers and radio broadcasts about the state of the investigation. He was even found one day taking pictures of the Starks crime scene with a young *Life* magazine reporter; neighbors had reported suspicious lights and sounds from the house when Gonzaullas and the woman were found.

While the local press, headed by the Texarkana Gazette, dubbed the suspected serial killer the "Phantom Killer" or "Phantom Slayer," national media clung to a different name: "The Moonlight Murderer." Because of this title, many believe that the murders were all committed under the full moon, when the nights were in fact at their darkest during the time of the crimes.

A Fruitless Investigation

The entire nation was on the lookout for a masked killer terrorizing young couples, with leads coming in from all areas of the South. In all, the authorities considered over four hundred separate suspects, but no one was ever charged with the attacks of that spring. While most of these suspects never received any public attention, the media caught wind of some of the more notable ones.

A middle-aged man from College Station, a Texas town several miles west of Texarkana, was at one point considered a prime suspect. He had previously been caught sneaking up on parked cars, typically with young couples inside, and brandishing a .22 rifle in order to threaten and rob them. While this man was never convicted of murder, many believed him to be the Phantom Killer based on the similar crime and weapon.

In Fayetteville, a young male graduate student of the University of Arkansas committed suicide. In the wake of his untimely death, a note was found containing a handwritten poem and confession to the murders in Texarkana. His military records showed he had showed "homosexual tendencies" during his time with the U.S. Navy, and at the time these tendencies were believed to be a mental disorder related to sexual crimes like rape or assault. Nothing of value ever came from this lead.

Several local residents accused an IRS agent of the crimes, seemingly because of his antisocial demeanor or because he had gotten on the town's bad side. Another man claimed to have committed the crimes during fits of amnesia. Neither of these claims resulted in an arrest.

In 1999 and 2000, several years after the last murder, an anonymous woman called surviving family members of the Phantom Killer's victims, claiming to be his daughter. She apologized for the actions of his crimes and begged for forgiveness from the families. There is speculation over whether these claims are valid, but many believe them to simply be a cry for attention. After all, the primary suspect of the Phantom Killer murders, Youell Swinney, never had a daughter.

Chasing a Criminal

During his time investigating the Moonlight Murders, Max Tackett, an Arkansas law officer, made a puzzling connection. Before each murder a car had been reported stolen and subsequently abandoned on the side of the rode. This information led police to believe that the Phantom Killer was using stolen vehicles to flee the crime scenes, and then dumping them before disappearing into the night.

The next car reported stolen triggered a police stakeout, with law enforcement hoping to find the killer connected to the vehicle. As police closed in on the stolen vehicle, Peggy Swinney was found to be driving. Police seized the car and took Peggy into custody, where she was questioned on how she came to possess the stolen vehicle.

Peggy revealed that Youell Swinney, a known car thief in Texarkana, had given the car to her, but that wasn't all she had to say. Peggy began telling police how Youell was the Phantom Killer, how he had assaulted and murdered all those couples, and how he had made her promise not to tell anyone. She included details of the crimes that had not been given to the public, information only known by police and the killer himself.

Before the police could move in on Youell Swinney, Peggy's story changed. She claimed that her previous confession was a lie, and that Youell was not the Phantom Killer after all. Eventually law enforcement discovered that Peggy and Youell had recently been married, making her unable to testify against her husband at all. While Youell remained an unofficial suspect, it seemed that the police were unable to touch him. But that changed in 1947, when Youell was arrested for auto theft.

At that time, Youell Swinney already had a long criminal record. He had been previously charged with counterfeiting, burglary, and assault, landing him in the Texas State Penitentiary for many years. After his release, he continued his work as a career criminal, but avoided capture for the time being.

During the investigation, police found evidence that Youell had owned a .32 Colt revolver, the murder weapon used to kill the second and third sets of victims, but that he had recently lost the gun in a failed card game. In hi home was also a shirt with the name "Stark" embroidered on the pocket, but it is unknown whether this shirt was actually connected to the Starks murder in the previous year.

With Youell in custody for auto theft, the police attempted to pin him as Texarkana's Phantom Killer. The man had a history of violence and sexual assault, and the record of stolen cars pointed toward his involvement in the murders. Youell never denied his innocence; he simply stayed quiet and refused to work with the police when questioned. A botched injection of "truth serum" during an interview in Little Rock, Arkansas, would eventually end the authorities' questioning of Youell regarding the Moonlight Murders. He was placed in prison for auto theft.

Youell remained in prison until 1973. Many of his cellmates recounted stories that Youell had told them, ones that included intimate details of the Phantom Killer's murder scenes and heavily suggested that Youell knew more than he let on. In 1994, Youell died a free man, never admitting to the Texarkana murders. To this day, most consider Swinney to be the Phantom Killer, even if he never served time for these crimes.

The Missing Woman

On June 1st, 1948, 21-year-old Virginia Carpenter departed Texarkana by train, on her way to her first semester of studying at the Texas State College for Women. She left Union Station at about 3PM, and headed for Denton, Texas and her new life as an educated woman. On the train ride, she met another student by the name of Marjorie Webster, who she shared a taxi with on the way to their dormitories.

Their taxi driver, Edgar Ray "Jack" Zachary, first dropped off Webster at the Fitzgerald dormitories, and then continued on to Brackenridge Hall, where Carpenter would be staying for the term. Zachary reported seeing Carpenter approach two young men in a yellow convertible outside the dorm, saying that she seemed to recognize them and was excited to see them. The next day, Zachary returned to the dorms to deliver some of Carpenter's luggage that she had forgotten at the station. He placed the trunk at the hall's front entrance and left, but no one ever claimed the luggage. That previous night would be the last time Virginia Carpenter was seen.

On June 4th, Carpenter's boyfriend, Kenny Branham, and her mother reported Virginia missing. After being brushed off by authorities, Mrs. Carpenter and other family members left for Denton late in the evening, hoping to help the police find Virginia.

Within several days, there were airplanes, motorboats, and on-foot search parties scanning the surrounding area for any sign of Virginia. Drivers of yellow convertibles were stopped and questioned, and Zachary was questioned by police and subjected to a polygraph test. Carpenter quickly became one of the most famous missing person cases in Texas, with her picture circulating across the country.

Before long, rumors started spreading back in Texarkana. Virginia Carpenter had personally known three of the Phantom Killer's victims, and some started to believe that she had a target on her back. Perhaps the killer had followed her from Texarkana to Denton, just another passenger on the crowded train. Or perhaps the killer was someone that Carpenter knew, like one of the men seen in the yellow convertible to night she went missing. Either way, many believe that this disappearance was connected to the attacks in 1946.

Countless sightings of Carpenter across Texas - riding in a car, buying groceries, or hitchhiking - continued to flow in, but no solid leads were ever discovered. By 1955, Carpenter was considered dead. She had been missing for seven years, and little hope remained of finding her. Despite this, tips continued to emerge on Carpenter's possible whereabouts.

In 1959, a wooden box was found buried with female remains inside that matched Carpenter's physical description. They were sent to Austin for examination, but the landowners soon confessed to digging them up from an old cemetery.

In 1998, a man called the police claiming to know where Carpenter's body was buried. He led police to the grounds of the Texas State College for Women, the school she was meant to attend, but the search came up empty.

Carpenter's disappearance causes some to doubt Youell Swinney's guilt. If her disappearance was a result of the Phantom Killer, the same man who brutally attacked at least three different couples, then this man could not be Swinney. At the time Carpenter went missing, Swinney was being held in prison for auto theft. Maybe Peggy Swinney had a hand in the disappearance of Carpenter, or her abduction was committed by someone other than the Phantom Killer, but it could not have been Swinney.

Phantoms Around the World

Some believe that the Phantom Killer simply moved his crimes to a new location, but it is likely he just inspired other killers to follow his pattern of attack. As the United States reached the height of violent crime and serial killers, attacks cropped up across the country and even abroad. The Phantom Kiiler's *modus operandi* (or M.O.) would become commonplace among serial killers in the coming decades, including the Zodiac Killer, Il Mostro, and the Son of Sam.

In 1946, a young couple was shot in Fort Lauderdale, Florida. Elaine Eldridge and Lawrence Hogan were parked outside Dania Beach when someone approached the vehicle and shot both victims with a .32 semi-automatic handgun. While the weapon used was not a Colt, it remained very similar to the one used in Texarkana. No fingerprints or footprints were found at the scene. With several similarities to the Texarkana attacks, many believed that the killer had relocated across the country. Texas, Arkansas, and Florida police worked together on the investigation, but no major connections were ever revealed to the public.

Located in San Francisco, the Zodiac Killer operated very similarly to the Phantom Killer during the late 1960s. He stalked young people in their vehicles and shot them with a revolver, and his identity remains unknown. However, unlike the Phantom Killer who personally avoided the media's attention, the Zodiac Killer was hungry for exposure. His main source of fame comes from sending cryptic notes to the Bay Area press, including four ciphers. Only one of these ciphers was ever solved, but it led the police no closer to identifying a suspect. These notes were examined top to bottom, in hopes of finding the true identity of the Zodiac Killer, but no leads were ever found.

Across the Atlantic Ocean, from 1968 to 1985, Florence, Italy was shook by sixteen murders. Dubbed Il Mostro or The Monster of Florence, the killer shot young couples parked alone in their cars with a .22 rifle. While four different suspects were arrested and charged with these murders throughout the years, the investigation has attracted scrutiny and many believe these men were actually innocent.

While the Son of Sam's identity is known today, his killings reflected those of the Phantom Killer and others. Operating in New York City in the mid 1970s, David Berkowitz killed six victims with a .44 Bulldog revolver. His attacks triggered the biggest manhunt in New York City, and for years women kept their hair short and avoided disco clubs for fear of being Berkowitz's next target. Like the Zodiac Killer, Berkowitz loved taunting the police and media with cryptic letters, where he promised to continue killing until he was caught. After his capture in 1977, Berkowitz enjoyed a bit of morbid celebrity for his crimes, which many reported he seemed to enjoy greatly. He remains in prison today, serving six life sentences.

While it is unlikely that the Phantom Killer actually relocated to be the Zodiac Killer or Il Mostro, some true crime experts believe it is possible. While the Phantom Killer was one of the first of his kind, looking back his killings were not exceptionally unique by today's standards.

It is easy to see how the Phantom Killer and his Moonlight Murders have shaped our ideas of killers today. Urban legends of a mad man stalking young couples in love, scratching on car doors and leaving bloody hooks behind, persist around campfires and in dark corners of the Internet. *The Town That Dreaded Sundown* might live among the likes of Freddy Krueger and Michael Myers, but it is a fictionalized retelling of the very real horrors that haunted Texarkana that year.

RAILROAD KILLER

They called him the 'Railroad Killer.'

Angel Resendiz earned the nickname because of his penchant for committing his crimes near railroads, using the rail cars as his own personal get-away system.

Committing murder after murder, he was able to elude both American and Mexican authorities for over a decade.

EARLY LIFE

A birth certificate found by the FBI listed his date of birth as August 1st, 1960. He was born To Virginia de Maturino in the town of Izucar de Matomoros in the state of Puebla, Mexico. His mother has stated adamantly that the correct spelling of his surname is Recendis not Resendiz although the killer would have over fifty different aliases throughout his lifetime.

Angel had spent his childhood years with relatives and not with his immediate family. According to his mother, he was sexually abused by an uncle and other pedophiles in the town of Puebla. He would spend his youth roaming the streets, robbing, stealing and sniffing glue. Relatives would later testify that Resendiz was routinely beaten as a child, one time being "jumped" by several other youths who beat him so bad that he bled through his ears. Resendiz would leave home for months at a time then suddenly return mumbling about a coming religious apocalypse.

Legal trouble came early for Resendiz as he was caught trying to sneak into the Texas border at the age of sixteen. This would become the first of numerous run-ins with border patrol agents until he finally made it into the United States, making his way to St. Louis and finding work with a manufacturing company under an assumed name. He even registered to vote with his false identification.

In September of 1979, at the age of nineteen, Resendiz was arrested for assault and car theft in Miami. He was tried and sentenced to twenty-years in prison but was released after only six years and sent back to Mexico.

But he wouldn't stay there for long.

Through numerous attempts of trial and error, Resendiz had learned not only to game the system but to enter and exit the United States with minimal detection.

He learn to use the rail-cars...

AN "INVISIBLE" MAN

Resendiz became so skilled at crossing the border without detection that he began charging for his services. He began to make a living as a human smuggler, transporting Mexicans across the border for a fee.

Resendiz soon developed a reputation for his smuggling skills, often being seen as a 'go to' person in his Ciudad Juarez neighborhood called 'Patria.'

He would make weekly crossings over the border, being arrested only intermittently. He would then be deported back into his native land only to ping-pong back and forth.

Finally, Resendiz would serve prison terms for his crimes. He would be arrested in Texas for false identity and citizenship, getting a year and half worth of jail.

Upon release in 1987, he journeyed to New Orleans and was arrested for carrying a concealed weapon. He received another year and half worth of prison time until parole.

He then went back to his old haunts in St. Louis where he tried to defraud Social Security and receive illegal payments. He got caught and served a three year sentence.

Resendiz then decided small-time burglaries were his deal. He once again illegally crossed the border, journeyed to New Mexico and was caught burglarizing a home. He was imprisoned for eighteen months and upon release he broke into a Santa Fe rail yard, being captured yet again.

"They should have called Resendiz the boomerang man," forensic psychologist Frank Lizzo said. "He knew how to play the game and seemingly had no fear of the system. The system never punished him severely enough for him to stop his crimes, let alone stop crossing the border."

After his last recorded deportation, the killings began.

THE KILLING FIELDS

"He probably started killing somewhere in his late 20s," Douglas said. "He may have killed people like himself initially – males, transients...(he) became angry at the population at large. What America represents here is this wealthy country where he keeps getting kicked out...(he) just can't make ends meet. Coupled with these feelings, these inadequacies, fueled by the fact that he's known to take alcohol, take drugs, lowers his inhibitions now to go out and kill."

Angel's list of victims began in 1986. Continuing to bounce in and out of the United States, he shot a homeless woman and left her for dead in an abandoned farm house. He had met the acquaintance of the woman at a homeless shelter and they became friends. They would later take a trip on a motorcycle together when he felt that the woman disrespected him.

Resendiz would then take out his gun and blow her head off.

The woman allegedly had a boyfriend whom Resendiz shot and killed as well. He said that he dumped his body in a creek between San Antonio and Uvalde. This killing has never been verified aside from what Resendiz revealed to the police during his interrogation sessions.

Five years later, Resendiz would kill Michael White because he was a "homosexual." Resendiz would bludgeon White to death with a brick and leave him in front of an abandoned home.

These were seemingly warm-ups for the more brutal crimes to come which would also include rape.

"Sex seemed almost secondary," FBI profiler John Douglas said when apprised of Resendiz's crimes. "(He is) just a bungling crook ...very disorganized."

Douglas would later concede, however, that it was this disorganization that worked in his favor. Like a true drifter, Resendiz' whereabouts became as elusive as a rational thought in his head.

"When he hitches a ride on the freight train, he doesn't necessarily know where the train is going," Douglas said. "But when he gets off, having background as a burglar, he's able to scope out the area, do a little surveillance, make sure he breaks into the right house where there won't be anyone to give him a run for his money. He can enter a home complete with cutting glass and reaching in and undoing the locks."

"He'll look through the windows and see who's occupying it. The guy's only 5 foot-7, very small. In fact...the early weapons were primarily blunt-force trauma weapons, weapons of opportunity found at the scenes. He has to case them out, make sure he can put himself in a win-win situation."

Resendiz would also leave his weapon of choice up to chance. Whatever the home would have, a statue a mantle piece, a butcher knife, that would become the instrument of murder.

FLORIDA KILLINGS

On March 23rd, 1997, Jesse Howell would be found bludgeoned to death beside the railroad tracks in Ocala, Florida. He was nineteen years old.

"When we got there," Sheriff Patty Lumpkin said. "We see what appears to be a young male, in his late teens or early twenties. Blood around the head area. You could tell by looking at him that he was dead. The first thing I do is make sure that we've got our forensics people on the way, on the medical examiners on the way, and all the investigators that we have called out or either there or en route."

"When those types of things happen it might have been someone who had fallen off a train," Lt. Jeff Owens said. "Or someone who could have been struck by a train."

The authorities quickly ruled out an accident, however, as they examined the body.

"It didn't appear to be an accident," Lumpkin said. "Because if he had been hit by the train the trauma would have been much more extreme. I've seen some deaths from trains and the initial impact from the train would have done more harm to the body."

The forensic team did determine that Howell's body looked as if he were the victim of blunt force trauma.

"We did see a baseball type of cap," forensic scientist Michael Dunn said. "It appeared to have blood on the inside surface of he bill. In addition, there was a pair of wire rimmed eye glasses and one of the eye pieces was missing, one of the lenses was out. This didn't look good either. As we moved closer, we saw that the victim had been dragged to that spot using just the blue jean material around the cuff (of his pants)."

Near the body, they found a brass and rubber coupling. This device was used to link one train car to another. It could also be used as a clubbing weapon.

"It had what appeared to be blood on it (the coupling)," Dunn recalled.

Howell still had jewelry on his person. He wore a gold cross necklace, a watch and a small amount of cash in his pocket. The police ruled out robbery as a motive.

The police did not identify Howell's body right off the bat. They did find a money wire receipt where some money had been wired from Illinois to Florida. The name on the receipt was of a woman named "Wendy."

Police tracked the money transfer to its point of origin which was all the way in Woodstock, Illinois.

Coincidentally, the authorities there were investigating the disappearance of Wendy Von Huben.

Wendy was missing alongside her boyfriend, the nineteen year old Jesse Howell.

"They advised me that they were investigating a John Doe," Woodstock Detective Kurt Rosenquest recalled. "Unidentified male."

Rosenquest then followed up with the investigating team in Florida, sending them the fingerprints and pictures of Jesse Howell.

The Ocala police would then positively identify Howell.

Jesse had met Wendy only months earlier. They had secretly planned to marry and went on a road trip with another couple.

The other couple, however, grew tired of Jesse and Wendy's constant bickering. They demanded to be let out of the car and left. Jesse and Wendy continued into Ocala, Florida where they ran out of money.

Wendy would call her parents in Illinois who would then transfer her $200 via Western Union. The couple would collect the $200 but would not return home.

"We checked Greyhounds," Rosenquest said. "Nobody matching their description ordered buses or train tickets back to the Woodstock area."

Tears were shed as Rosenquest informed Howell's parents that their teen son had been murdered. The investigative team then turned their attention to the disappearance of Wendy.

They held out hope because there were issues between her and Jesse, thinking that perhaps she simply ran off to be by herself.

Police scoured the surrounding areas and used helicopters in all directions around the railroad tracks.

They would find nothing. There was no DNA left behind on Jesse Howell's body either.

Papers and fliers with Wendy Von Huben's information was distributed all throughout Florida up through Illinois.

Authorities also began interviewing the transient population that lived along the railroad tracks.

Two and a half months later, however, Wendy's parents would receive a phone call.

"The phone rang," Rosenquest recalled. "Wendy's father answered the phone. The girl was crying. She said 'I'm sorry. I love you.'"

She would tell the father she was two hours away from Woodstock at a gas station. The father asked for the phone number on the pay phone she was calling from and she said that there wasn't any before hanging up.

The police were not certain that the phone call came from Wendy so they immediately headed out to the gas station where they believe the call took place.

Police tracked down the surveillance video of the gas station. On the video, a woman that physically resembled Wendy entered the gas station.

The phone records, however, revealed that the call did not come from the gas station where the surveillance video revealed a woman who allegedly was Wendy. It came from another gas station where there were fliers posted of Wendy.

Someone had played a cruel hoax as Wendy's parents had added their home number to the fliers

ONE-LEGGED BOB AND A CHANCE DISCOVERY

A year went by without any sign of Wendy.

There was some ray of hope, however, as the railroad authorities called the Ocala police and informed them that the received information from a member of one of the homeless camps. They had a man in custody named "One Legged Bob" who was traveling with a girl and may be responsible for the murder of her previous boyfriend.

"'One Legged Bob' was your typical homeless person," Owens said. "Kinda scruffy. Hadn't shaved in a few days. He had a prosthetic leg that helped him get around. For someone who you might consider crippled, he was far from crippled."

Owens would spend the next eight hours interviewing the only lead he had, a one legged homeless man.

After the grueling interrogation, Owens realized that he had the wrong suspect.

By sheer chance, however, Patty Lumpkin heard about someone they dubbed the "Railroad Killer" during a class she was taking at the FBI.

"They called him the Railway Killer," Lumpkin recalled. "The Angel of Death. He was killing people. Leaving them near the railroad or he was killing them at homes or locations that were close to the railroad.

The FBI knew the Railway Killer as Angel Resendiz.

"We knew that Angel Resendiz was a person that rode the rails across the country," FBI Agent Mark Young said. "We were worried where he'd wind up next. So we decided to make him a top ten fugitive. Maybe the millions of eyes of the public would tell us something."

The strategy worked.

"He was one of the most vile, evil persons that I had ever dealt with," Young said. "It was like every time you turn around there's another murder."

Owens and Lumpkin hoped to talk to Resendiz to query him about Jesse Howell's murder and Wendy Von Huben's disappearance.

"The attorneys representing him at the time in Texas stopped us," Owens said. "They wanted to protect their client from talking. Any defense attorney who represents a criminal will generally tell the person to stop talking to law enforcement."

Resendiz was placed on death row and Texas had a fast execution rate. The two detectives worried that they would lose their chance to interview Resendiz and connect him to the crimes in Ocala.

Owens and Lumpkin decided to mail Resendiz a letter, respectfully asking him if they could interview him. The letter was written in a formal manner and even addressed him as "Senor."

To their surprise, Resendiz responded back and granted them an interview regarding his involvement in Jesse's killing and Wendy's disappearance.

During their meeting, Resendiz was quick to admit that he had killed Jesse. The detectives deliberately withheld information about the killing, holding back details that only the killer would know. But when Resendiz described using a brake coupling from one of the trains, they knew they had their killer.

But they needed to find out what happened to Wendy.

In a follow-up letter, they promised him immunity from prosecution if he agreed to talk. It was a moot point by then as he was already on death row but the detectives still needed permission from Wendy's family to go through with the interview.

In order to receive some sense of closure, the family agreed to the immunity.

"When we get to the prison," Lumpkin said. "We see him coming down the hallway. He (Resendiz) has a waist belt on. It's an electric shock belt and he's chained to the belt. He's just a mild-mannered person but remember that a psychopath or a sociopath doesn't have any feeling. I mean he had dead eyes. He had no feeling in that body. He didn't care about anything."

Resendiz would reveal that he was heading south for work when the train stopped and he spotted Jesse getting off the train for a smoke.

"Resendiz told us that he killed Jesse with a piece of the train coupling," Lumpkin said. "And Wendy was asleep on the train when this took place. And then when they went down the road further somehow he talked Wendy into getting off the train."

Resendiz then raped and strangled Wendy to death.

Resendiz drew a map of where had left Wendy's body. He described burying her in a shallow grave near a canopy of trees. Resendiz would remember that she had a book in a back pack and an army style jacket that he used to cover her fresh grave.

Police would return to the site and were able to locate where he buried Wendy's body. Almost three years after the murder, everything the killer described was still there. The book. The jacket.

And Wendy's body.

"When Wendy ran away she had a small engagement ring," Owen said. "And she had a Winnie the Pooh wristwatch."

The detective would bring those items back to Wendy's parents.

KENTUCKY RAILROAD MURDER

In August of 1997, Resendiz would make his way from Ocala, Florida to Lexington, Kentucky. It was there he would stalk two young college students.

Holly Dunn was a 20-year old junior at the University of Kentucky and it was there she met Christopher Maier.

"Chris Maier was my very good friend," Dunn recalled. "He was just the nicest, kindest man. We decided that we wanted to be more than friends then we started dating. We dated for about three months."

"Chris and I were attending a party. We decided that the party wasn't very fun so we went to go talk a walk by the railroad tracks. We sat down and talked for awhile and when we got up to leave a man came out from behind an electrical box. He had a weapon that he used on Chris. It was some sort of ice pick or screw driver. Something sharp. I guess our immediate thought was he's going to rob us. That's when we realize he wants money we start thinking 'okay, well, you could have our credit card, you can have our ATM card, you can have our car.' Then he started tying up Chris' hands behind his back. And then he came over to me and he took off my belt and that's when I started thinking he doesn't want to rob us."

After tying up Holly, Resendiz then pulled Chris by the shirt across the railroad tracks and into a ditch.

Holly would follow on her knees, pleading for him to stop whatever he was about to do.

"Lie down," Resendiz said, his voice soft but menacing.

"Everything is going to be okay," Christopher said to Holly as Resendiz dragged him into the ditch.

"Shut up!" Resendiz commanded as he gagged Christopher with a sock.

Resendiz then walked off into the darkness. The frightened couple did not know what the psychopath had planned.

"Then he comes with this rock," Holly recalled. "There was no warning, he drops this rock on Chris' head. I'm just thinking 'what just happened?' I don't even know what just happened."

"You don't have to worry about him anymore," Resendiz said to Holly as he got on top of her.

"I went into survival mode, I'm thinking, I mean he's gonna kill me. I may as well fight. I'm gonna fight. He unties my feet and climbs on top of me. I start to kick and scream and hit him but he held that knife or ice pick (to my throat) and said 'look how easily I could kill you.' I stopped everything and then he raped me."

"I memorized his face," Dunn said. "I stared at him and memorized, he had a tattoo on his arm, I was thinking if you have any scars I'm gonna remember your scars, I'm gonna remember your face,I'm not gonna forget it because if I live through this I will get you."

Resendiz completed the sexual assault of Dunn before smashing her head with a rock.

"He hit me five or six times in my face," Dunn recalled. "I think I put my hand up and then I turned over and then he hit me five or six times in the back of my head. He hit me hard. He was trying to kill me. I think I laid there and he thought I was dead."

Resendiz did think she was did as he threw the rock down and ran away from the crime scene.

Holly would suffer severe facial trauma but miraculously survived the attack.

"I had a broken jaw," Dunn said. "Broken eye socket and cuts on the back of my head that they had to staple shut and then I had cuts on my face."

She woke up in a Kentucky hospital, surrounded by family members.

"Everyone was told not to talk about Chris to me. I just said 'Chris is dead, isn't he?' And my Dad actually is the one I said that to and he was like 'yes, he died.'"

TEXAS TERROR

Resendiz would travel to Texas via train and in October of 1988 he flopped down in Hughes Springs. He would enter the home of 87-year old Leafie Mason, attacking the woman with an iron and killing her.

Two months later, Resendiz would sneak into the home of Dr. Claudia Benton, a thirty-nine year old medical researcher who lived in a suburb of Houston near the railroad tracks.

Again, it was a case of a home being to close to the train tracks. The train would provide the perfect cover for the sneaky Resendiz as he realized that the sound of the rail-car racing by would allow him to break in homes without being heard.

He applied the same technique with Benton, breaking into her home, raping then killing her.

Police would find the doctor face down on the floor. Her bedroom soaked in blood, ransacked for any valuables.

He head had been covered in a plastic bag while her body had been covered in a blanket.

"It appears that she (Claudia Benton) was sleeping," recalled Ken Macha, former police sergeant. "He was able to get in and picked up a bronze statuette from the mantle in the living room. He was relentless in beating her. The skull fractures themselves would have been enough to kill her. She was then stabbed in the back with a very large butcher knife."

"Resendiz was brutal, sadistic," said former West University police chief Gary Brye.

Fingerprints and DNA evidence would link Resendiz to the crime. The problem was they could catch the man that Texas Ranger Drew Carter referred to as "a walking, breathing form of evil."

EVADING POLICE

Seven months later, Resendiz would continue to avoid capture. He remained in Texas, riding the rail cars until coming into the town of Weimar. He would break into the home of Pastor Norman "Skip" Sirnic and his wife Karen. Resendiz smashed a jack hammer into both of their heads, killing them instantly. He would then rape the body of Karen postmortem.

"He would watch these places," prosecuting attorney Devin Anderson said. "He would watch them, wait for them to go to sleep, get in their house and he would strike them before they would even wake up. I thought we have got to catch this guy."

The DNA found at the scene of the Sirnic murders would match those left on Benton. The FBI then realized they had a highly mobile serial killer on the loose...someone who could kill in one town then appear in another town miles away and kill again.

Resendiz was also smart. He would constantly alter his appearance. He'd shave his head. Then his mustache. He'd be clean shaven one week. Unkempt the next. He would wear glasses one week. No glasses the next.

Authorities could not get an accurate description of him other than the fact that he was small.

Resendiz was also able to take advantage of the lack of a coordinated computer system that gave law enforcement the ability to cross-check fugitives. After the Sirnic murders, Border Patrol had encountered Resendiz near the El Paso border but did not find him on the wanted list.

They then deported him back to Mexico.

Within 48 hours, Resendiz was back across the border to resume his killing spree.

"Our computers told us that he was nothing of lookout material," said C.G. Almengor, a supervisor at the border. "We really wish he had been in the system so we could have caught him."

Resendiz would be deported no less than seventeen times over the course of his rampage. At no point did authorities make the connection because of his changing appearance, use of different aliases and the lack of a connected system to document illegals trying to come across the border.

A PREFERENCE FOR TEXAS

Noemi Dominguez was a graduate of Rice University who had just recently quit her job as an elementary school teacher to pursue a master's degree.

She was described as "the sweetest, nicest teacher – a darling who went the extra mile."

Fueled by hate, Resendiz would break into Noemi's home and rape her before killing her with a pick ax. He then stole her car and drove to Schulenberg, Texas where he would kill Josephine Konvicka with the same pick ax.

He would leave the weapon embedded in Konvicka's head as well as leave his fingerprints all over the home. He was more than just sloppy, he was getting cocky. He left a newspaper article that described his crimes as well as a toy train...a reference to his nickname as the "Railroad Killer."

Resendiz was also meticulous in approaching his victims.

"He undid the light in her (Noemi's) car," Anderson said. "So when he opened the door it wouldn't come on. That's who were were dealing with. Someone who really knew how to sneak around. Who really knew how to avoid detection."

"He kept killing people. He would not stop. In his mode of transportation, using the railroads was brilliant because they couldn't be monitored. I mean there's thousands of trains and millions of miles of tracks all over the United States."

"I felt hopeless at the time. Because if you're willing to sleep in a train or you're willing to sleep in a field, you can stay lost for a long, long time and I didn't think we were ever going to catch him."

Later that month, Resendiz had journeyed to Illinois, reaching the town of Gorham. He would break into the home of 80-year old George Morber and his daughter Carolyn Frederick. Resendiz would tie Morber to a chair and shoot him in the back of the head with a shotgun. He then raped Carolyn and smashed the shotgun across her head with such force that the weapon broke in half.

Both Morber and Frederick would die from their injuries.

The FBI placed him on their Top Ten list.

They then recruited his common-law wife, Julietta Reyes, and brought her into Houston for questioning from her hometown of Rodeo, Mexico.

Reyes complied with police requests, turning over over ninety-three pieces of jewelry that her husband had mailed to her from the U.S.

Relatives of Noemi Dominguez claimed thirteen pieces. George Benton was able to identify some pieces of jewelry as belonging to his wife as well.

Police would then locate Resendiz's half-sister, Manuela Karkiewicz, who lived in New Mexico. Initially, she refused to cooperate. She worried that the FBI or the police would kill her brother. But Carter convinced her to talk Resendiz into giving himself up.

The FBI knew that Resendiz had made his way back to Mexico after the murders in Illinois and was hiding in his hometown neighborhood of Patria.

Carter was able to get a rapport with Manuela. He convinced her that Resendiz would receive "personal safety while in jail, regular visiting rights for his family and a psychological evaluation."

"I came away with the impression that they (Resendiz' family) definitely had an understanding of right and wrong ... and knew now that what Maturino Resendiz was accused of doing was heinous and wrong ...," Carter said. "Manuela, especially, came across as a woman of strong faith. There was a very deep emotional strain and burden placed on her in this investigation. She had to make some very difficult choices that impacted her and her family. And, in the end, her actions alone speak to her character."

Carter spent weeks talking to Manuela who in turn "worked a miracle."

They got the serial killer to surrender.

On July 12th, Manuela would receive a fax from the district attorney's office in Harris County which formalized everything that Texas Ranger Carter had promised.

The word passed from Manuela to another relative who acted as a go-between with Resendiz. The relative than came back later that evening and said that Resendiz would surrender in the morning at 9 a.m.

Texas Ranger Drew Carter would accompany Manuela and a spiritual adviser to meet with Resendiz on a bridge that connected El Paso, Texas to Ciudad Juarez.

"When I saw that face there was a little bit of excitement there because I finally said, 'This is going to happen,'" Carter recalled as he remembered Resendiz appearing on the bridge with his dirty jeans, muddy boots and blank facial expression. "He stuck out his hand, I stuck out my hand, and we shook hands."

Resendiz would then surrender to the Texas Ranger.

DEATH PENALTY

Resendiz' attorneys knew that their only hope would be an insanity defense. The Mexican government also got involved, lobbying authorities to spare Resendiz the death penalty

"Insanity was the logical defense because no one wants to believe that there is someone out there who would do things like that," Anderson said. "That was the thing that worried me the most about the case was that jurors would just throw up their hands and say nobody in their right mind could do what he does."

"The thing about what a life sentence with Resendiz would have been, he would have enjoyed it. I mean he would have had pen pals. He would have given interviews if they let him, I mean he would have loved it. And I knew that. And he didn't deserve to live after what he did just didn't. He caused so much pain, so much heartache and so much terror, that's what the whole focus of the trial had to be."

George Benton, the husband of Claudia, would vehemently criticize the Mexican government who support his appeals and domestic opposition to the death penalty.

"(He)looked like a man and walked like a man. But what lived within that skin was not a human being."

"He was small," Anderson said when she first saw Resendiz in the courtroom. "Maybe five- foot five. His forearms though, were roped with muscles. He was scary. Even though he was small you could feel he was dangerous. He looked like a wild animal who'd been caught."

Resendiz looked "timid" in the courtroom and spoke of himself in religious riddles. He claimed he was Jewish and didn't seem effected when he was informed that the prosecution was aiming for the death penalty.

"I don't believe in death," Resendiz, said. "I know the body is going to go to waste. But me, as a person, I'm eternal. I'm going to be alive forever."

The defense said that Resendiz' crimes were caused by head injuries, drug abuse and a family history of mental illness. He has a delusional perception of the world as he believes that he can cause earthquakes, floods, and explosions and that God told him to kill his victims whom they believed to be evil.

He made a living stealing things from his victims and having his wife sell them in Mexico. "That was his job," Anderson said. "And for recreation it was killing the people who lived in the house."

"He was a very intelligent person who worked the system and knew exactly what kinds of things to say to get that defense to work."

The jury, however, would find Resendiz guilty after one hour and forty-five minutes of deliberation.

He was sentenced to die via lethal injection.

"He made it very clear during my conversation with him that he deserves to die," Owens said.

"I want to ask if it is in your heart to forgive me," Resendiz said in his final words. "You don't have to. I know I allowed the devil to rule my life. I just ask you to forgive me and ask the Lord to forgive me for allowing the devil to deceive me. I thank God for having patience with me. I don't deserve to cause you pain. You did not deserve this. I deserve what I am getting."

Resendiz then prayed in Hebrew and Spanish before drawing his final breath.

House of Horror : The True Story of Rosemary West

Mary Gilmore

Unfortunately, it's not unusual in this day and time to turn on the news and hear a warning about a new serial killer roaming our streets. It's horrifying and hard to comprehend what could possibly make a person commit such heinous crimes. What is wrong with this person that drives him or her to commit such an act? The truth is that people have searched for the answers to that question for a very long time. Unfortunately, it still remains a mystery for the most part.

Rosemary West is one of those baffling cases. We will look deeper into her life and learn how her inner demons progressed to becoming one of Britain's most notorious and sadistic serial killers, taking the lives of at least 10 young women and girls.

Most of the information obtained by the authorities came from her husband and partner in crime, victims who escaped or were permitted to leave, and a great deal from her own children. Rosemary has offered very limited insight into the story, even to this day.

Remarkably, she did not act alone in committing these grisly deeds. This story is immensely complex, which I will attempt to sort out and then tie it all together with the union of Rose Letts West and Fred West in their vicious killing spree. There will be accounts of child abuse, rape, sexual deviance, torture, and murder. Rosemary West's crimes were so horrendous; it may be difficult for some of you to read.

Rosemary West's Early Life

Rosemary's mother came into her room one morning to wake her for school. Rosemary probably knew by the familiar expression on her mother's face that this would be one of those mornings that fills her life with constant dread. As she gets dressed, she begins preparing herself for what she knows is probably about to occur.

As she walks into the kitchen, breakfast is the last thing on her mind. Instead, she braces herself for the punishment she is about to receive. Don't misunderstand, Rosemary hadn't done anything wrong, but her father didn't need a reason.

His kind of punishment wasn't a time-out or a swat on the behind as most children receive. His were the kind that affect a child for a lifetime. Rose has no idea whether she is about to be beaten or if she'll endure other horrors that her father is known to inflict.

That is a likely scenario in the life of Rosemary West. Her father was a paranoid schizophrenic. The mental illness along with other problems, made life for her, her mother, and her siblings a nightmare. The abuse was bad enough, but what made it even more terrifying was not knowing from one minute to the next when or why her father's rage would erupt.

As a result of her home life, Rose made bad grades and became overweight. To make her situation worse, she was teased and bullied at school, giving her no relief from the continuous damage to her self-esteem.

There's a possibility that Rosemary's destiny was sealed much earlier in her life. It's not surprising that Rosemary's mother suffered from severe depression. The illness was so debilitating that she received electroconvulsive therapy several times while Rosemary was still in the womb, one of which occurred just before Rosemary's birth. There were some that thought this therapy was the reason for Rosemary's frequent outbursts of anger as well as her inability to do well in school.

Most of us would be unable to imagine a childhood such as the one led by Rosemary West.

Why do They Kill?

There are no exact traits of a serial killer to help us understand what drives them to kill. Some of them come from a two parent loving home while others have divorced parents. Some had abusive parents and others had loving parents.

Some think it's due to a head or brain injury sometime in their life; however, most people that have had brain injuries do not become killers. The majority of serial killers are men who act alone. Rosemary is not only a woman, she also had a partner in her life of crimes. Female killers and couples represent only a small percentage of serial killings. The Federal Bureau of Investigation did a symposium, which was comprised of 135 experts who have dealt with serial killers in various ways to determine commonalities of serial killings. They determined that there are no definitive common traits. However, the central nervous system is constantly developing in adolescence, which determines a person's social coping system. That is, they develop the way they interact with their peers such as in negotiation and compromise. If it does not develop adequately, it can result in violent behavior.

It would be safe to say that the events of Rosemary West's childhood could be a factor in the choices she made later in life.

Rosemary's Life Before the Murders

Rosemary Letts was the fifth child born to Bill and Daisy Letts in Devon, England on the 29th of November in 1953. She normally went by the shorter version of her name, Rose. As we've seen, Rose's childhood was unlike most other children's. In pictures of Rose at a younger age she had an ever present smile on her face. You wouldn't guess that she was going through hell within the walls of her home.

The Letts family lived in Northam, a charming seaside town in Devon. Neighbors thought of Bill Letts as a nice man; however, they must have thought it strange that they rarely saw his children. When they did, the children were mainly seen walking around in their garden. One neighbor stated that they really didn't seem to be playing at all. They were just walking around and rarely seen outside the walls of the garden.

What they didn't know was that the children weren't allowed outside the walls and were afraid to play because they were forbidden to get dirty.

Although Rose's father constantly punished the children including Rose, he was not as physically abusive with Rose as with his wife and the other children. It was thought that he didn't physically abuse her as much as the others because he thought there was something not quite right about her.

Some people thought that he didn't hurt Rose as much because he was using her for his sexual pleasures instead. Others speculated that Rose learned at a very young age that she could control her father's anger by using sex.

Rose's mother Daisy, eventually left her father. She moved out of their house taking Rose and the other children with her, freeing them from the abusive environment. Remarkably, after a brief time, Rose moved back in with her father who resumed sexually abusing her.

One day, as Rose waited for a bus, she was approached by a man. Rose described him as a dirty man who had disgusting green teeth. She and the man struck up a conversation and even though his appearance was repulsive by most people's standards, Rose became attracted to him. The man's name was Fred West.

West was raising his daughter and stepdaughter at that time so Rose began babysitting the two girls. In addition, Rose and Fred also became a couple.

Fred's Early Years

Fred West, the son of Walter and Daisy West, was born in Much Marcle, England in 1941. He was the second of their six children. Growing up, he was considered to be a nice boy. They appeared to be a normal family, however, Fred's upbringing was perhaps even worse than Rosemary's. According to Fred, the motto around his house by his father was, "Do whatever you want, just don't get caught."

Fred would later reveal to police that incest was a common occurrence in his household. He said his father regularly had sex with his own daughters. Fred also claimed that his father introduced him to bestiality. In addition, it was thought that his mother Daisy took his virginity when he was 12-years-old. Not surprising, Fred did not do well in school and dropped out at the age of 15. Two years later, he was involved in a tragic motorcycle accident. He received a broken arm and leg and a fractured skull. The head injury put him in a coma for eight days. Afterward, his family claimed that thereafter, he frequently become enraged without warning. Amazingly, two years later, he received another head injury. In this instance, he fell from a fire escape causing unconsciousness for 24 hours.

Fred's history of child abuse and head injuries would certainly coincide with the conceivable characteristics of a serial killer.

At the age of 20, he was caught and arrested for molesting a 13 year-old girl who subsequently became pregnant. He was convicted, but for unknown reasons he was not sentenced to prison. The reason is possibly because the girl's parents and Fred's parents were friends. Even with his family's propensity for deviant sexual acts, they had recently decided to try their hand at getting religion, therefore, they disowned Fred after this latest incident.

Fred had problems keeping a normal job. He landed a construction job; however, he was caught stealing. In addition, he continued to get caught molesting more young girls. It's amazing how he could still be roaming the streets even back at that point.

Shortly after, when West was around 21, he ran into a former girlfriend named Catherine Costello. She was better known as Rena, which was the name she used while prostituting and the name stuck. In addition, Rena was an accomplished thief. Nevertheless, even with her reputation, she was described by neighbors and other acquaintances as a very nice person and an exceptionally good mother.

Even though she was already pregnant with another man's child at the time, things heated up between her and Fred again and they married about two months later. The baby girl was born in February

1963 and was named Charmaine. Rena had another child by Fred a year later and named her Anna Marie. You will hear the names of these two girls in a shocking context later in the story.

Unbelievably, someone gave Fred West a job driving an ice cream van. This wouldn't seem a proper job for Fred the child molester to say the least. For Fred, it was the perfect job with young girls running after him. It was an ideal way for him to find victims.

While working at this job, a four-year-old boy ran into the street in front of his van and the child was killed. After this incident, even though the death was accidental, Fred feared people in the area would seek retribution for the boy's death. He thought it would be in his best interest to move away.

At the time, a woman named Isa McNeil was caring for the West's children. Additionally, Rena had become friends with a young woman named Anne McFall. They all moved with Fred to *The Lakeside* caravan park in Bishop's Cleeve, Gloucestershire, which is where Fred would later live with Rose.

With Fred's sadistic habits still intact, there were soon problems in this odd household. Fred insistently pushed his warped sexual necessities onto all three women. It became too much for his wife, Rena, and the children's nanny, McNeil, so the two of them moved to Scotland. On the other hand, the other woman, Ann McFall, had warmed up to Fred and stayed behind. Besides, she had already become impregnated by him.

Fearful of Fred, Rena and Isa's planned was to keep their departure secret from him and sneak away. Unfortunately, McFall told Fred, which enraged him. He allowed them to leave, but not with the two children, so the two women fled to Scotland. Rena returned frequently to visit her children.

After that, McFall began to pressure Fred to divorce Rena and marry her. Apparently, this didn't set well with Fred. When she was eight months pregnant with Fred's child, she completely vanished. She was never reported missing, but her body was later discovered in a field minus her fingers and toes, which had been removed and were missing. Fred was left to care for his daughter and stepdaughter.

The Evil Duo Unites

Around this time is when Fred met Rose at the bus stop. It was at the time when Fred was caring for his step-daughter and biological daughter, so Fred already had at least the one murder of Anne McFall under his belt when he met Rose. Rose then began taking care of the two children.

When they first got together Rose was only 16-years-old and Fred was 12 years older at 28. Her father absolutely disapproved of the relationship. He threatened West that if he didn't leave Rose alone he would call Social Services due to Rose's young age. That was ironic since her father had been having sex with her himself for a long time. Of course, that was most likely the reason he didn't want her to go.

Nevertheless, Rose moved in with Fred and they lived together as a family with Fred's two daughters. After only about two months, they married she moved in with him at *The Lakeside Caravan Park* in Bishop's Cleeve, Gloucestershire, where Fred had lived with Rena and Anne.

Of course Fred, a man of few scruples, soon introduced his young and damaged wife to a sadistic world of pornography and urged her into prostitution. Due to Rose's demoralizing childhood, it didn't take a lot of urging for her to become caught up in his world.

Not one to hold down a regular job, Fred's contribution to the income was mainly by thievery. He wasn't very accomplished at that either and was frequently caught and arrested. It wasn't long before he was sent to prison for 10 months, leaving young Rose in charge of his two daughters.

To make matters worse, she had become pregnant and gave birth to her daughter, Heather, in 1970 while Fred was still in jail. Being young in addition to having mental problems, caring for three children was a tall order for Rose and she didn't handle the situation well, to say the least.

To add to the pressure, seven-year-old Charmaine, began to be unruly and Rose was unable to cope with it. Years later, according to the other child, Anna Marie, it was not unusual for both girls to receive severe beatings; however, no matter how bad the beating, Charmaine refused to cry. This infuriated Rose so it's no surprise that Charmaine didn't seem to be around any longer after that.

This is thought to be when Rose committed her first murder. Rose's tendency to lose her temper most likely caused her to loss control and kill Charmaine. Apparently, Rose hid the girl's body, because it's known that Fred disposed of the body after he returned from prison.

Fred would hold this over Rose in the future. On one of the occasions when Rose's father tried to convince her to leave Fred and come home, Fred made a remark that was something like, "Come on now Rose, you know what we have between us." For someone that didn't know Fred, it would sound like an expression of love. More than likely with Fred, it was his not so subtle way of saying, "You can't leave. I have too much on you." She later told her parents that Fred would do anything, including murder.

Fred's first undertaking after returning from jail was to dismembered and dispose of Charmaine's body. For whatever sick reason, as with Anne McFall, he removed her fingers and toes and then buried her. This became the normal process in Fred's body disposal. It was later speculated that Fred and Rose were possibly involved in Satan worship. It is thought by some that removing the fingers and toes of their sacrifices was typical for Satan worshipers.

The next time Rena Costello came to visit her daughter it naturally created a problem when she discovered her daughter's absence, thanks to Rose. As you can imagine, Rena was not happy about her missing daughter and demanded some answers. Therefore, Rose and Fred must have decided that Rena would have to go as well. So this visit to see her little girl resulted in Rena's demise as well. Minus her fingers and toes, she was buried in a field close to the Caravan Hotel where Rose and Fred still lived.

That meant a total of at least three people had already lost their lives courtesy of Fred and Rose West. One each for Rose and Fred and now Rena by both of them.

A brief time later, Rose gave birth to their second child, Mae. They bought a large two-story house in Gloucester; however, there was not much money coming in. Fred started putting up panels in the rooms to create multiple bedrooms called bedsits. They were tiny rooms, which didn't fit much more than a bed. They began renting out these rooms for extra income; however, the rooms served another purpose as well.

By this time, Rose's fulltime career had become *prostitute*. They also began working other women out of the house. One of the rooms labeled "Rose's Room" was dedicated to Rose for turning tricks. Outside the door was a red light, which was lit when the room was in business. The children knew they were not to disturb when the red light was on. The room also came complete with a peephole, which was Fred's method for watching his wife in action and for making videos.

Both Rose and Fred had come from a family where incest was normal. It was not unnatural to them when Rose's own father occasionally came to their house to have sex with her.

In around October of 1972, Rose and Fred hired Carol Owens as a new nanny for their children. She told her story years later stating that Fred and Rose attempted to bring her into their twisted lifestyle. Not wanting any part of it, she soon left their house.

A few weeks later, as she was walking home, Fred pulled up beside her and offered a ride. The next thing she knew he hit her on the head. When she awoke, her hands were tied and Fred was in the process of taping her mouth.

She was told that if she tried to resist, Fred would call in his friends and let them have their way with her and she would then be killed.

They said they would bury her under the paving stones outside their home along with hundreds of other girls. Terrified, she didn't attempt to resist.

Unbelievably, they allowed her to leave the next day and she proceeded to file charges on them. Fred somehow managed to convince the court that the sex was consensual. In addition, Owens decided that testifying against these two could be an unhealthy choice.

The couple was given a meager fine on a charge of indecent assault and then released. She would be the last victim that the Wests' would allow to leave alive.

Years later, she regretted not testifying. She felt that if she had, it could have saved the lives of numerous women and girls and she was most likely correct.

One day, Fred and Rose arrived home and their neighbor, Elizabeth Agius, was outside. She had become friendly with the couple, so Fred stopped for a chat. Just in conversation, she asked what they had been doing, so Fred proceeded to tell her exactly what they had been up to.

He said they were cruising around looking for young girls. He must have felt he needed to explain why his wife would go along with him on such an outing. He said they figured the girls would see Rose and wouldn't be scared to get in the car. She would later say that she thought he must be joking...he wasn't.

Meanwhile, Fred was busy redecorating the cellar. One of the prostitutes that worked in the house later told authorities that she saw black suits, masks, chains, and whips down there. Fred had created his own torture chamber.

Anna Marie, Fred's remaining child with Rena Costello, was the first to be brutalized in Fred's torture chamber. She was bound, gagged, and violently raped as Rose watched. She was only eight-years-old at the time and this treatment would continue for years.

Eventually, Anna Marie moved out of the house to live with her boyfriend, which quite possibly saved her life. Again, letting her go would prove to be a bad move for the Wests later in court. As one of the survivors, a considerable amount of the horror stories came from her. After Anna Marie's departure, Fred's attentions naturally turned to his daughters Heather and Mae; however, Heather wanted no part of it and resisted. Understandably, she was unable to keep it to herself and told a friend about the horrors happening at home. This would seal her fate, but Fred later claimed to police that her death was accidental.

The life of Rose and Fred West continued filled with the unimaginable. They would go on to have a total of seven children who were born in a short time span. It is believed that three are by Fred, one is by her own father, and the remaining three are from her clients. It almost seemed that their reason for having children was so Fred and Rose would have someone to torture at the times when no one else was tied up in the cellar. You can certainly say with certainty that Fred and Rose West were definitely not loving parents.

The One's That Didn't Survive the Terror

Over the next few years, the abuse of the West's children continued as did the murders of others. At some point, Fred went to work at a slaughter house. It was thought that this is when his already violent habits became even more gruesome. It could have been a factor in his fascination for dismembering his victims.

It is believed the next victim was Lynda Gough who was a personal acquaintance of the West's. She enjoyed participating in some of their sexual activities by sharing sex partners with Rose. However, for unknown reasons she later vanished. Gough's mother came to the West's house looking her daughter and was told that she moved in order to pursue a job. While she was speaking to the woman, Rose was wearing some of Linda Gough's clothing.

Carol Ann Cooper, only 15-years-old, is thought to be the next victim. She disappeared while walking home from the movies.

Evidence showed she died by strangulation, was dismembered, and buried in the garden.

Lucy Partington was in town visiting her family and a friend over the Christmas holidays. She went to the bus station to take a bus back home and most likely Fred, being one to hang out at bus stations asked her if she wanted a ride. As Fred and Rose planned, it is thought that the only reason she let them even approached her was due to the presence of Rose.

It is thought that they kept Partington in captivity for about a week after she vanished because poor Fred showed up at the hospital about a week later with a large laceration needing stitches. Authorities think he received the cut while cutting up Partington.

Shirley Hubbard went missing when she was returning home from Droitwich. There was definitive evidence of her torture. Her head was completely wrapped with tape with only a short rubber tube in her mouth to breath.

Juanita Marian Mott was a former tenant of the Wests'. Her torture was obvious. She was gagged with a binding made of socks, tights, and a bra, which were all stuffed inside each other. She was also tied up with clothes line rope looped around her thighs, arms, wrists, and ankles. This was done with the rope going back and forth around her horizontally and vertically until she was completely immobilized. She also had a rope with a noose, which most likely suspended her from the rafters in the cellar.

Shirley Anne Robinson was one of the prostitutes that worked out of their house who had sexual relations with both Fred and Rose. She became pregnant by Fred, at the same time Rose was pregnant by one of her clients.

Shirley began to get the idea she would like to replace Rose, which is not advisable in this family. Rose demanded that she had to go. She and her unborn child were dismembered and buried in the back garden. The cellar was full of bodies by this time and the back garden became the new burial grounds.

Therese Siegenthaler was a hitchhiker in route from London to Ireland. Some of the evidence showed that like Partington, she was kept alive for close to a week during which time she was likely tortured and raped.

Allison Chambers was the last known non-related victim. She was killed in 1979.

Their oldest daughter, Heather Ann West, was the last known victim. Fred claims he killed her by accident. His story of the "accident" went something like this. He told police that Heather was being extremely insolent so he had to slap her. She then started laughing at him so he was forced to grab her by the throat to stop her from laughing. He said that unfortunately, he must have grabbed her too tightly because she began to turn blue and stopped breathing. He tried to revive her by putting her in the tub and running cold water on her, but it didn't work.

He then removed her clothes and attempted to put her in a garbage bin, but she didn't fit. Back into the tub she went so he could make her smaller, but he first strangled her with a cord to make sure she was dead. He told police he didn't want to start cutting her up and then have her come alive on him.

He also closed her eyes before he started cutting. He said he couldn't dismember her while she was looking at him. He must have been hearing a strange sound because he told police he found the source of a noise when he cut off her head. He said it was a horrible and unpleasant sound like scrunching. He also said that after cutting her up, she fit quite nicely into the garbage bin.

She was later put in a hole that the West's son, Stephen, had dug with the intention of it becoming a fishpond. Fred put Heather in the hole and built a patio over it. Stephen had unknowingly dug the grave for his own sister's burial.

Police also believed that they killed 15-year-old Mary Bastholm in 1968, though they never found her body. The Wests' son Stephen, later told authorities that he believes Bastholm was one of his father's earlier murders because his father boasted about it.

The Evidence Begins to Surface

Oddly, they violently murdered many of their victims, but then set others free after they had finished using and abusing them. Naturally, some of them went to the police.

The released victims were some extremely lucky women to say the least. Their reports finally got the attention of a Detective Constable named Hazel Savage. Savage was also familiar with Fred West and his arrests for thievery and child molestation through the years since the time he was married to Rena Costello.

Fred videoed an incident in which he raped Anna Marie while Rose held her arms. Anna Marie told friends about her home life who in turn told their parents. This and other information got back to Savage.

This enabled the Detective to obtain a warrant to search the West's property. It was the beginning of the needed evidence to finally remove these damaged and dangerous monsters from the unsuspecting public.

Fred was arrested and charged with rape and sodomy of a minor and Rose for assisting in the rape of a minor. Amazingly, Fred and Rose West were still not suspected of murder. At this time, the younger children were removed from the home.

Due to the evidence found in the home, Detective Savage had the suspicion that there was more going on here and she began digging deeper into this strange family. She had a feeling that there was something suspicious concerning the whereabouts of their daughter Heather and she was determined to find out.

For instance, it was noticed in the videos of the West's and their children that was seized from their home that Heather was never present. Also, in interviews with some of the children, they said something that should not come from the mouths of children.

Apparently, there was a common joke around the West house. Fred told the children that he would buried them under the patio with their sister Heather if they didn't behave.

Unbelievably, the case fell apart when two of the main witnesses decided not to testify. Detective Savage continued questioning the children repeatedly to no avail. Fred and Rose had programmed them and put enough fear in them by then that they would no longer say anything to help the case.

However, the evidence together with case workers reporting the family joke about their sister Heather kept Detective Savage searching. It also appeared that another child, Charmaine, was missing as well. Eventually, Savage put together enough evidence to obtain a warrant to dig on the Wests' property.

Soon after that, Rose answered the door to find the police with warrant in hand. She quickly called Fred to tell him the police were about to dig on their property and they're looking for Heather. It turned out that Fred would be of little help because it took him four hours to get home. He came up with some excuse about passing out due to inhaling paint fumes at work.

Could it have been that Fred was busy disposing of evidence such as fingers and toes or perhaps he had a burial he had not gotten around to completing. That will never be determined.

They began searching the house in addition to excavating the garden in February 24, 1994. The dig was originally intended to search for the body of the daughter Heather, which they soon found. Fred was brought in by the police for questioning the next day. He surprised the police by confessing to the murder of his daughter Heather and he repeatedly told police that Rose knew nothing about it.

Fred and Rose must have been up all that night getting their stories straight. It is thought that Fred assured Rose he would take all the blame and she shouldn't worry. Fred was good to his word, at least in the beginning.

Meanwhile, after the attending pathologist began inspecting the bones of Heather, he brought it to the attention of the police that there was an extra leg bone indicating the presence of at least one other body.

After that discovery, Fred decided he should do some damage control by telling police the location of Alison Chambers and Shirley Robinson's bodies. He hoped this would prevent them from doing any more digging.

It was first thought that Fred did this to avoid being categorized a serial killer, which is someone that kills more than three people. Unbelievably, as it turned out, Fred wanted the police to stop digging because he didn't want his cherished home to be torn apart any further.

Nevertheless, they continued and began to find more human bones. Rose was not arrested until around March 4, 1994. Even then, it was only for sex offenses. Fred had trouble deciding for sure if he wanted to protect Rose after all. He would go on the recant his confession that he killed Heather and then later changed his mind again saying Rose was innocent.

In Britain, prisoners are sometimes assigned an "appropriate adult", which is someone that assists and basically befriends the prisoner. This was normally done for juveniles; however, Janet Leach was assigned to Fred. Leach didn't know she was about to become the confidant of a serial killer.

It turned out that Fred became comfortable enough with Leach that he soon told her the whole gory story. She pointblank asked him if there were more victims. Fred responded that there were six more and went on to draw a sketch of his house and garden complete with the locations of the graves.

Fred knew exactly where they were located; however, he had some trouble remembering all their names. He recalled one that had a scar on her hand; therefore, Scar Hand became her name. Another he called Tulip because he thought she was Dutch, although she was actually Swiss.

Fred was now on a roll and confessed to the murders of his ex-wife Rena Costello and ex-lover, Anne McFall. He told leach that he dumped them nearby his childhood home. He then confessed that he buried his step-daughter Charmaine, Fred's child that Rose killed, close to the hotel where they lived in Gloucester. Strangely, Fred would admit to the murders, but he would not admit to the rapes.

Meanwhile, Rose continued to play the role of an innocent woman, denying any involvement in the murders. She went so far as to act horrified at the actions of her perverted husband. When Fred attempted to contact her, she snubbed him not wanting to have anything to do with such a despicable person.

After making bail, Rose moved into a halfway house with her son Stephen and her daughter Mae. The police were not convinced of her innocence and bugged the house. Nevertheless, Rose stuck to it and never spoke of anything that would involve her in murder. Only charges of sexual offense remained against her.

As can be imagined, the town of Gloucester was flooded with the media. The attention had a tremendous impact on the small town. The West's house became known by the appropriate name "The House of Horrors". The residents were in disbelief that this unimaginable crime spree had gone on in their town for 20 years.

The Trial

As it turned out, Fred took the easy way out. He hanged himself in his jail cell by tying together bed sheets leaving Rose to deal with the whole state of affairs.

She was finally charged with 10 of the murders since Rena Costello and Anne McFall were before she was on the scene. She went to trial in October of 1995.

One after another, witnesses took the stand and told their shocking stories. One of the highest drama moments of the trial came with the testimony of Fred's oldest daughter, Anna Marie. She was on the stand for two days. At one point she looked her stepmother straight in the eye as she told a story of sexual abuse and torture that began when she was a little girl of only eight-years-old.

She recalled the incident when she was so savagely raped by her father while Rose held her arms. During the incident, Rose was telling her how lucky she was to have parents to show her how to please her husband when she gets married. She said she was hurt so badly that she couldn't attend school for several days. She also recalled a day that her father strapped her down and raped her while he was home for a quick lunch break. These were only two of the many horror stories she lived.

The second day of her testimony was delayed for several hours because she took an overdose of pills the previous evening.

Another person that offered a wealth of damaging testimony was Fred's *Appropriate Adult* and confidant, Janet Leach. However, she became so stressed that she suffered a stroke during the trial causing another delay. It wasn't until later after the trial's end that Leach could tell police the entire story that Fred confided in her.

One of the key witnesses was Carol Owens who was one of the girls they brought home under the pretense of being a nanny. She was allowed to leave, but only after she endured their sadistic sexual torture. Needless to say, she had tales to tell.

Another witness who is still referred to as Miss A was lured to the West house and saw two naked girls who were being held prisoner. She watched as they were tortured and raped. She was then raped by Fred and sexually assaulted by Rose. She was one of the lucky ones that left that cellar with her life.

It wasn't hard for the jury to come back with a unanimous verdict of guilty on 10 counts of murder. Rose received life in prison.

The Aftermath

The "House of Horrors" at 25 Cromwell Street in Gloucester where nine bodies were found was demolished in October of 1996; however, there seemed to be a curse that affected many of the people associated with Rose and Fred West.

John West, Fred's brother, hanged himself while awaiting his trial for the rape of his own niece Anna Marie.

Anna Marie continued to suffer from the memories of her distorted childhood. In 1999, she attempted suicide by jumping from a bridge. She was rescued, leaving her to live another day with the memory of the horrors from her past.

Stephen West, the son of Rose and Fred, attempted to commit suicide in 2002 in the same manner as his father and uncle by hanging himself. However, it wasn't meant to be because the rope broke.

The actual number of murders will remain a mystery. During his interrogation by the police, Fred stated that there were two more bodies buried in shallow graves that they would never find.

He also told them there were 20 other bodies spread around in various places. He claimed he would show the police the location of one body each year. One wonders if he knew at that time that he would later take his own life and wouldn't be following through with that promise.

Fred took any other secrets he had in his evil little mind with him to his grave. After that, Rose wasn't interested in discussing the matter any further.

According to an article in the DailyMail, dated February 2014, even though Rose West filed for a couple of appeals after she went to prison, she has now decided she never wants to leave her top security jail cell at Low Newton jail in Durham and why would she, her cell is equipped with TV, radio, CD player, and private bathroom. She has never confessed to committing any murders.

Authorities know the women and girls were tortured, raped, killed, dismembered, and buried; however, they don't know the details of many of those crimes. Rose has been asked by numerous people to give those details, but she refuses.

Conclusion

This is an account of actual facts; however, it hard to believe that it's anything other than a fictional horror story.

Even after hearing about the disturbing childhoods of both Rose and Fred West, it's difficult to understand the extent of their warped minds. Even more disturbing is the fact that two people that are this broken can find one another and carry out their evil deeds together.

This story brings us no closer to the answer of what drives serial killers. Both Rose and Fred were abused as children mainly by their fathers; however, it was young women and girls that were the focus of their punishment.

There have been books and a movie made about them to show us how this horrific story unfolds. However, only in our minds can we come close to conjuring up the evil that occurred within the walls of 25 Cromwell Street. We may never know the full extent of the terrors that transpired.

The fact that Fred West is gone and Rose West will never see the light of day should make us all sleep a little more soundly.

Printed in the USA
CPSIA information can be obtained
at www.ICGtesting.com
LVHW041107280924
792329LV00001B/125